OMF 73/74/33/1/2/3/5/5/52   4/30/74

FREDERICK C. KLEIN
and
JOHN A. PRESTBO

Henry Regnery Company · Chicago

Library of Congress Cataloging in Publication Data

Klein, Frederick C.
  News and the market.

  Bibliography.
  1. Stock-exchange and current events. I. Prestbo,
John A., 1941-   joint author. II. Title.
HG4551.K576   332.6'42'0973   73–20313

Published by Henry Regnery Company
114 West Illinois Street, Chicago, Illinois 60610

Manufactured in the United States of America
Library of Congress Catalog Card Number: 73–20313
International Standard Book Number: 0-8092-9029-4

Dedication

To Carol and Darlene

Contents

Preface

You are driving home after a day's work and you turn on the radio. It's time for the business news. "The stock market rallied today on news of such and such," the announcer says, or, "Stocks declined today on news of this or that."

That seems to make sense, you think. But when you reconsider it, you realize that every day there is good news *and* bad news, the market either goes up or down, and it must be tempting for a broadcaster or newspaper writer working under deadline pressure simply to select the day's events that matched the direction of the market. Does the market react to news or doesn't it, and, if so, how?

As reporters for a national business newspaper, we have asked the same questions. When we looked to the almost endless number of books and articles that have been written to explain why stocks behave the way they do, we found little that was satisfying. So we decided to have a go at it ourselves.

It certainly makes sense to believe that the stock market

ix

responds to the news. Movements of the market as a whole, and of the stocks that make it up, spring from the decisions of thousands of investors. These people—be they steely-eyed fund managers on Wall Street or little old ladies in Dubuque—read the newspapers, watch television, and so on, and presumably are affected by what they see and hear. If the United States seems to be getting along well with other nations around the globe and the economy seems to be functioning smoothly, it stands to reason that they will feel well-disposed towards sharing in the bounty. If the opposite conditions obtain, a savings and loan account or a hole in the ground might seem more secure.

Moreover, the way that stock prices advance depends greatly on communications. If a man at a racetrack finds out something about a horse that improves its chances of winning, he does well to keep the information to himself because others who are similarly informed will bet on the horse and drive down his return if the horse wins. In contrast, if a man thinks a stock will go up and buys it, it behooves him to convey his view to others in hopes that they, too, will buy it, bidding up its price. (On Wall Street, this is known as "telling your story.") And there are plenty of publications that are eager to let their readers in on a good thing.

Investors of bygone days put high importance on news; otherwise, the Rothschilds and news-gathering pioneer Julius Reuters wouldn't have sent pigeons crisscrossing nineteenth-century Europe with news bulletins strapped to their legs. In 1855 word of the siege of Sebastopol reached London, and "an early Reuters messenger boy, taking a message to the Stock Exchange, was put on a chair, cheered, and a collection made for him," relates Graham Story in *Reuters*.

The same opinion prevailed in the early United States. During the Civil War, a forum set up in New York to speculate in gold was not named the Gold Exchange but Gilpin's News Room. In the 1880s, the notorious wheeler-dealer Jay Gould bought himself a couple of New York newspapers so that his takeover raids on companies would be treated kindly by at least a portion of the press. In the great bull market of the 1920s, traders and newsmen were known to make arrangements under which a newsman would write glowingly of a stock a trader had purchased, increasing its value and enriching both. That sort of thing is believed to be less prevalent these days, but examples still surface now and then.

Today, of course, we are deluged with news from all sides, and often the problem seems to be not how to get it but how to escape from it. A common complaint of the modern businessman is that he can't even begin to digest all the business-related information that comes across his desk and still have time to do his job.

Indeed, the very abundance of news seems to have resulted in its devaluation in the eyes of some prominent Wall Streeters. "Practically the only time spot news is really good for stocks, and vice versa, is when it is a complete surprise," writes investment adviser Gerald M. Loeb. He goes on: "The Kennedy assassination of 1963 would be a good example: No one could possibly have had advance information. It was a shock, and the market reflected the shock."

"News is merely one of the many factors having a bearing on the course of stock prices, and in many instances it is not the most important one," writes Louis H. Whitehead, limited partner in the brokerage firm of Hornblower & Weeks—Hemphill Noyes. "The items which constitute what is generally termed *news* have a lesser impact on the price of a single issue or group of stocks than any one of a large number of factors."

As these statements indicate, those who regard news as having little impact on stock price movements share two notions: a very limited view of what constitutes news and a great confidence in the ability of key stock market participants to anticipate important developments before they occur and make their trading decisions accordingly.

We, on the other hand, choose to define the news broadly as *anything*, fact or opinion, that finds its way into the news media. Obviously, much of the news is not germane to the stock market, but we think much of it is, as we will spell out later in more detail.

We agree that a good portion of the news—including many of the developments that might be expected to have the greatest impact on stocks—unfolds in a more or less regular way. It is well established that the economy as a whole moves in cycles of expansion or contraction stretching over months and even years, so it would be reasonable to assume that there would be a flow to the news that would reflect these movements.

But we seriously question whether this flow can be discerned far in advance by even the most sophisticated investor-readers. Recent stock market history certainly indicates that Wall Street's pros aren't nearly as omniscient as they might have us think; the manner in which many professionally managed mutual funds were burned in the bear markets of 1966 and 1969–70 has been widely documented.

Although examples abound of the sort of news involving individual stocks that might have been predicted by traders but wasn't, one should suffice. On December 8, 1972, Time Inc. announced that it would stop publishing its money-losing *Life* magazine three weeks hence. *Life*'s demise had been anticipated for years, but the day of Time Inc.'s announcement the company's stock shot up by more than 10%; and it posted a 30% gain by year-end. A short-term move, of course, but what's wrong with a short-term profit?

Our effort to investigate the effect of news on stocks divides into five parts.

Part I, comprising our first three chapters, is introductory. Chapter 1 looks into the nature of the modern stock market and some influential current theories of stock price movements as they relate to the news. Chapter 2 catalogs the major outlets for financial news in the United States. Chapter 3 tells how business news originates, in the hope that such knowledge will help the reader in evaluating it.

In Part II—Chapters 4, 5, 6, and 7—we lay out a framework for quantifying the news and show how this measure has related to broad stock price trends over much of a seven-year period. These chapters contain the heart of our argument that the news indeed makes itself felt in movements of the market as a whole.

Part III focuses on the impact on stocks of three kinds of issues: war, U.S. presidential elections, and environmental pollution, the latter representing a larger group of social issues. The three topics were chosen because of their dominant role in the news over the past several years and because they vary in terms of time: Wars break out irregularly; presidential elections take place every four years; and social issues are ever with us. In Chapters 8, 9, and 10, which deal with these subjects, we adopted a qualitative approach to news evaluation as the only one feasible.

We retained the qualitative approach in Part IV—Chapters 11, 12, and 13, which deal with how news in or about 1972 affected the stocks of Curtiss-Wright Corp., General Mills Inc., and Winnebago Industries Inc. These stocks were picked because they followed a representative variety of price patterns: Curtiss-Wright rose a lot quickly and then dropped some; General Mills forged ahead slowly but steadily; and Winnebago collapsed after a spectacular rise. In the chapters that recount their journeys, we paid special attention to when the stocks moved in relation to the news about them—a vital concern to investors.

We don't pretend to have hit on any system to beat the market. That wasn't our intention. But we do hope to show that close attention to the news can make you more alert to the kind of currents that can improve your ability to invest profitably in common stocks.

Acknowledgments

We would like to thank the numerous people who gave us assistance and support in preparing this book. Many of our colleagues at the *Wall Street Journal* gave us the benefit of their experience in helping us understand some of the subjects we covered. David Elsner and Terry Brown helped with the research, and Jon Laing and Harlan Byrne supplied valuable criticisms of the text.

Bill Cox, Jr., a friend, also helped with the research. Brokers and security analysts at Chicago Corp. and William Blair & Co. participated as volunteers in preliminary work that gave us insight into how stock market professionals viewed the news. Ronald Strauss of Mesirow & Co. also was helpful in this respect.

John W. C. Johnstone, professor of sociology at the Chicago campus of the University of Illinois, assisted us in building a study design for news evaluation. Professor Fischer Black of the University of Chicago Graduate School of Business reviewed the text and made valuable suggestions.

NEWS
AND THE
MARKET

Part I

Introduction

1

The Changing Market

SOMETIMES the stock market reacts to news and sometimes it apparently doesn't. Sometimes a certain news development will cause scarcely a ripple, while a similar bit of news at another time will send prices plunging or soaring. Sometimes the market—or an individual stock—moves in the opposite direction from what the news would seem to indicate.

Part of the explanation of this perverseness lies in the character of the market, which affects the way stocks react to news.

Some things about the market have remained essentially the same since brokers got an auction going in 1792 under the buttonwood tree in front of 68 Wall Street. Stocks are still traded by open outcry on the floor of the exchanges, and there still is a buyer for every seller and a seller for every buyer, even though thousands of miles may separate them.

But many things are different. For one, the market is a lot bigger now. Instead of a handful of traders in lower Manhattan and other handfuls in Boston and Philadelphia, there were at the beginning of 1973 an estimated 32.5 million Americans who owned common stocks directly and 100 million or so more who indirectly benefited or suffered from market action through pension plans, insurance policies, and the like. This was five times the number of people in the market in 1952, although the U.S. population grew by only 39% between those years. By 1975, some 40 million direct investors are predicted and by 1980, 50 million.

The market is growing on the other end, too, as more and more companies issue stock to be traded. Despite the merger and acquisition boom of the 1960s, stock listings on the New York Stock Exchange rose to nearly 1,500 by the end of 1972 from 1,200 a decade earlier. Listings on the American Stock Exchange, which attracts newer, more venturesome companies whose stocks are more speculative, rose to more than 1,400 from about 1,000 in the decade ending in 1972.

Even more speculative are many of the stocks traded over-the-counter or exclusively on regional exchanges (most of whose volume is in shares also traded on the Big Board or Amex). Some of these stocks have such a small float of publicly held shares available for trading that even tiny shifts in supply or demand—such as those sparked by a news story—can result in major price moves.

Even so, investors are quite interested in these stocks. On the Midwest Stock Exchange, to pick one regional market, the number of issues traded jumped from 475 to 740 in the 1952–72 period. And eventually, the computerized quote system operated by the National Association of Security Dealers for over-the-counter stocks will have a capacity for 20,000 listings; in 1972 it carried about 3,500.

The growth in the number of stocks has accelerated the flow of financial and business news. The tremendous increase in the number of investors—many of whom demand more information than investors of earlier years—has intensified the interest in this kind of news. It is competed for more vigorously and analyzed more closely than ever before. Its influence, in short, is greater.

March of the Megabucks

The stock market in the late nineteenth and early twentieth

centuries was characterized by a succession of individual giants, such as J. P. Morgan, who were so wealthy and influential that they could personally move the market or even rescue it from precipitous declines. But today the movers and shakers of the market are the institutional investors—mutual funds, pension plans, insurance companies, bank trust departments, foundations, investment counsellors, and even corporations trying to turn a buck on idle cash. These institutions accounted for nearly 70% of the volume on the New York Stock Exchange in early 1973, up from 30% a decade earlier, while individual investors' shares of volume dropped to about 20% from more than half. In some stocks, more than 90% of the trading is institutional.

Institutional ownership of outstanding shares on the Big Board grew from about 30% in 1963 to almost 50% in 1973. From an estimated $310 billion in 1973, the total equity holdings of financial institutions is predicted to grow to $714 billion by 1980 and to $5 trillion by 2000.[1]

These enormous sums of money, the megabucks, have an explosive influence in the market. When several institutions decide to make the same move in the same stock at the same time, "It's like the Green Bay line hitting a revolving door," one broker has commented. "There's nothing to do but stay out of the way and hope the door can be repaired."[2] The impact is especially noticeable when megabucks are pulled out of stocks rapidly. *Business Week* noted:

> When a stock falls out of institutional favor, it can plummet like a stone—with a disturbing impact on the over-all tenor of the market. A classic case is Levitz Furniture Corp., which plunged from $47 to $33 in less than a half-hour last Sept. 29 [1972]—a fall of nearly 30%. Virtually all the selling was by institutions as it was when Wrigley was hit for 30 points in one day, and when Handleman Co. lost 51% of its value in a single trade.[3]

The Levitz drop was precipitated by a report of unexpectedly low earnings—the kind of news that has always been important but in these days of institutional dominance can pack a terrific wallop in the market. That's because the money managers who control the megabucks often react to news in the same way.

"There are strong structural reasons why institutions tend to go one way or the other massively and almost in unison," said Sidney Homer, a prominent Wall Streeter. "They talk together. They know what others are thinking and doing. They know their fellows can dominate near-term market trends. Furthermore, if their mistakes are shared with the best people in the biggest institutions, they are not censured as severely as if their mistakes arose from bucking a generally accepted opinion."[4]

Implicit in this explanation is the desire of many money managers to outperform the market, a feat that makes them look very, very good. They acquired this desire from a group of brash young "gunslingers" who came to Wall Street in the 1960s and competed fast and aggressively to get the best ride for their customers' money. The gunslingers rode high for a while but turned out to be human after all when their stocks tumbled along with everyone else's in the bear markets of 1966 and 1969–70. Still, they left an indelible mark on what had been the safe and slow world of institutional investing. Performance is the name of the game, the gunslingers told their admiring listeners, so don't be afraid to get into a stock, ride it up, get out, and move on to something else. Most megabuck managers didn't emulate their gunslinger colleagues to the fullest, but even the stodgiest began twirling their portfolios with more gusto, with an eye on the performance ratings.

If institutional influence is noticeable when megabucks move into or out of a stock, it also can be detected when institutional managers choose not to react to the news. The *Wall Street Journal* told of such a case on September 5, 1972:

> Last Wednesday, Shapell Industries, a West Coast homebuilder with a strong rate of earnings growth, projected roughly 20% profit gains in both 1972 and 1973. With its stock selling at only a little over 10 times its 1973 forecast, it wouldn't be unreasonable to expect some enthusiastic buying to greet the glowing projections, considering Wall Street's hunger for growth companies with paltry price-earnings multiples.

So what happened?

The stock managed only a tiny ¼-point rise.

The reason—which isn't any secret—is the Street's widespread disenchantment with the homebuilding industry.

Says one money manager: "The homebuilding stocks are cheap. But they're going to stay cheap for a while because you can't get a handle on the extent of the expected decline in housing starts. There's no risk, but you're not going to make big money."

Another more subtle effect of institutionalization is the influence that the megabucks exert on companies. Institutions owned about 50% of the outstanding shares of such glamor stocks as IBM, Xerox, and Avon Products, and from 20% to 40% of many others, according to a Securities and Exchange Commission study in 1969. In their book *The Silent Partners,* Daniel Jay Baum and Ned B. Stiles say that institutional investors' big blocks of voting stock

... can strongly influence if not ultimately determine management action. They [the institutions] have the ability, the expertise, to evaluate management intelligently. They have the financial resources which management seeks for its capital needs and which can be brought to bear, if necessary, against management.[5]

The authors noted that there was an embryonic movement in the law—through court decisions mostly—to put the dominant shareholder in a fiduciary relationship to minority shareholders. If the so-called Doctrine of the Dominant Shareholder is widely adopted, a big institutional investor would have to conduct its activities in such a way as to be in the best interests of smaller shareholders.

Wall Street in 1973 also was moving toward curtailing the growing influence of institutions on the market. Among the suggestions were limiting the amount of stock an institution can trade in a day and how much it can own in a single company, and requiring advance announcement when a big block of stock is to be traded.

For the time being, though, the increasing role of institutional investors has made the market more sensitive to the news than it used to be. Because many money managers think and act alike, their buy and sell decisions sometimes produce volatile reactions in stock prices, which in some cases can influence the psychology or tone of the whole market.

Thus, investors can judge a stock's potential for a sudden, substantial reaction to a piece of news by the amount of institutional interest it attracts. The higher the involvement, the more sharply the price can rise or fall in reaction to news.

More Market Research

Along with the rise of institutional investment activity has come a proliferation of Wall Street research. According to the Financial Analysts Federation, there were 16,000 to 17,000 security analysts in the United States in early 1973, up from around 13,000 five years earlier. About half of these were actively engaged in analyzing stocks, while the rest were in executive positions or were managing investment portfolios. The growth in the number of analysts leveled off in the bear market of 1970 but picked up again in succeeding years.

The profusion of research has sharpened investors' perceptions of the news by providing them with a framework with which to judge future developments. A financial analyst visits a company, talks to its officers, checks its operations, investigates its financial condition, and considers its prospects. Then he writes a report, usually predicting the company's future earnings and making a trading recommendation of some sort. At that point the news about the company no longer floats in a vacuum but takes shape in a context that investors can understand. Generally, the more research done on a company and its stock, and the more widely the analysts' reports are circulated, the more potential impact news may have on price action.

"You and I can own the best potential growth stock around, but if nobody else knows about it, and wants to own some, too, we might as well kiss it off because it isn't going anywhere," sums up Harry C. Piper, chairman of Piper, Jaffray & Hopwood Inc., a Minneapolis-based brokerage firm.

Analysts' research isn't the only means of establishing an investment context for news; over a period of time, companies themselves can do the same thing through their news-disseminating activities. But it is nonetheless true that whether their work is thorough and accurate or not, the analysts are instrumental in shaping investors' attitudes and expectations, which in turn affects their judgments of the importance of the news. For example, a report that XYZ Company earned $1 a share will have much less impact on the price of XYZ stock if everybody was expecting $1 than if everybody had been looking for 50 cents or $1.50. We'll touch on this point again in subsequent chapters.

Theories of the Market

Analysts and other stock market sophisticates, as well as some not-so-sophisticates, use a variety of theories to explain what makes the market as a whole tick and to guide their investment decisions. None of these theories is infallible, but almost all of them at one time or another have shed some light on the direction of the market and have accurately predicted its next move. Some of the more popular theories have enough adherents to move the market if they buy or sell together.

For our purposes, we'll classify the theories, or, more accurately, approaches to the market, into two types—those that consider the news important (or at least take it into account), and those that don't.

The Mystical Approach

First the don'ts. In this camp are the astrologers, who predict market action based on positions of the planets—Jupiter, Saturn and Uranus are said to swing a lot of weight on Wall Street. A somewhat different tack taken by one pair of "analysts" was to keep track of energy emissions from the solar system, which they said influenced mass psychology and, thereby, the stock market. Still others count sunspots or listen for messages from the spirit world, which presumably knows in advance how everything will turn out. There's even a half-serious notion that stock prices rise and fall in concert with the length of women's skirts.

The Technical Approach

The technical approach, which in its pure form eschews news as a worthy consideration, is more respectable.

Technicians contend the price of a stock is already the total of every positive and negative factor that anyone who is in a position to act on a stock knows about. They believe that by studying the price movements of the market or an individual stock they can predict likely future movements. Pure technicians aren't interested in a company's earnings, dividends, or even what the company makes. One technician went so far as to board up his office windows to shield himself from worldly stimuli, and he avoided reading anything but stock tables in the *Wall Street Journal* until an issue was at least two weeks old.

That's probably not what the originator of the technical approach had in mind. He was Charles H. Dow, founder of Dow Jones & Co. and the first editor of the *Wall Street Journal*. (Dow Jones and Mr. Dow's Dow Theory parted company long ago, and there is no present connection between them.) Dow didn't think the news he purveyed was unimportant, but he did believe that it more affected the ripples and waves of the market—the short-term and intermediate movements—than the market tides—the long-term bull or bear movements. His theory, which actually was formulated by a succeeding editor of the *Journal*, William P. Hamilton, consists in large part of determining whether the long-term trend of the market will be up or down.

From that point, technicians have developed an array of price-chart interpretations, indicators, indices, and whatnot. Many of these methods are very complicated attempts to discover whether there is more selling pressure (supply) than buying pressure (demand) in the market, or vice versa, and what the "smart money" is doing. Some technical analyses can be carried on only with computers, as, for instance, the Intraday Intensity Index. In brief, this system involves a daily computer study of the intraday price action of all securities listed on the Big Board and the Amex. This index is bullish when the majority of stocks close at their intraday highs on increased volume, or close at their intraday lows on reduced volume. Other technical indicators gauge the ratio between the number of stocks that advance during a period and those that decline, or the ratio of trading volume on the more speculative Amex to the Big Board's.

For all this statistical paraphernalia, Wall Street continues to insist that there aren't any rich chartists and that the technical approach is more of an interpretive art form than a science. Still, technical analysis has gained considerable popularity in recent years, partly because some megabuck gunslingers have put in a good word for it. In fact, some institutions have come to react similarly to certain technical signals, which has added considerably to technicians' credibility.

Ironically, however, the developing dominance of the institutions also has caused serious problems for the technicians. Many of the technical indicators are based on the differing investment decisions of the sophisticated and the naive, but these relationships have veered off their historical norms as the public's influence has dwindled. As a veteran Wall Street observer points out, "One afternoon's unloading by these big dealers can wipe out a chart pattern that may have been months in the making."[6]

Many investors who use the technical approach aren't so wedded to it that they close their eyes to news developments; instead, they combine the two in a sort of cross-check system, as is evident in this advice to neophyte investors:

> Watch the reaction to news items. If a stock has been advancing, and a good earnings statement is put out or a bullish statement is issued by one of the company officers but the stock does not advance, this would indicate a weak technical position of the individual stock. You are likely to get a reaction.
>
> By the same token in a declining market, if a poor earnings statement or a bearish statement by [an investment advisory] service or company officer is published and the stock refuses to go down, it generally will be a buy for at least a good rally.[7]

In short, the technical condition of a stock or the market also can be part of the context governing whether the news will have little or great influence on prices.

The Fundamental Approach

There are three market theories that *do* consider news an important influence and together their adherents outnumber the technicians manyfold. By far the most important of these is the fundamental approach.

Fundamentalists—including most security analysts and almost all average-guy investors—believe market action reflects developments in the real world of business. If a company is making and selling more and more widgets, increasing its sales and earnings, the price of its stock will go up. Likewise, if widget sales slump and earnings decline, the price of the stock will drop. Profits now and in the future are the pivotal considerations in the fundamental approach.

The theory also is applied to the general economy, where such factors as interest rates, tight or loose credit, international monetary equilibrium, industrial production rates, retail sales, and consumer spending are among the important fundamentals. These and other economic measures are used to construct models that project where the economy will be in a few months or a few years, given certain conditions and trends. Some of these models also project results for certain companies and the likely performance of their stocks.

The most sophisticated fundamentalists can be just as arcane as the technicians. They try to figure out what the price of a stock *should* be, based on analysis of the fundamental factors plus subjective evaluations of such matters as management, the overall health of the company, and projected future earnings. Depending on the actual price, a company's stock thus is judged to be underpriced or overvalued. There are a variety of methods and formulas used by analysts to arrive at these conclusions, but like everything else connected with predicting the market, none is consistently accurate.

In the fundamentalists' view, whether stock prices are high or low in relation to their true value—whatever that is—has much to do with how the market or a stock will react to the news. "While a high cost of values in itself does not start a [price] decline, it does mean that the market must be fed with good news and encouraged by hopes that values will increase in the future. Markets that are cheap on the basis of values can stand on their own feet; those that are overvalued are sensitive to unfavorable developments," wrote the late Ralph A. Rotnem, a noted commentator.[8]

The fundamentalist approach influences the market's reaction to news in another way, too. The practice of fundamentalism produces expectations of what is to happen, and news is judged on the basis of how it relates to those expectations. Thus, a company may report higher earnings and other cheerful news, but if the good news doesn't seem sufficient to make the expectations come true, the price of its stock is likely to drop, or at least stop rising. News that causes expectations to be revised is especially potent.

The old market cliché, "Buy on the rumor, sell on the news," is one manifestation of this focus on expectations. It means that anticipation of a development is likely to move prices more than confirmation of it. Often, in fact, the expectation of an imminent and desired event—peace in Vietnam, for example—will cause stock prices to rise, but the arrival of the event itself precipitates a decline. That's because the fulfillment of a widely predicted expectation can create uncertainty about what comes next.

Which brings us to another point. For an expectations-oriented fundamentalist, be he neophyte investor or sophisticated analyst, uncertainty is the worst possible condition. He can cope with good news or bad news, but unsettling news frustrates him to the point that he doesn't know whether to buy, sell, or hold. If the uncertainty is prolonged, many fundamentalists are prone to withdraw from the market altogether. At the very least, uncertainty lowers the prices that fundamentalists are willing to pay for their expectations.

The Random Walk Theory

Random walk theorists are the anarchists of the market. They contend that price movements are for all practical purposes unpredictable, and therefore there is no systematic relationship between what happened yesterday, what is happening today, and what will happen tomorrow. Predict earnings or plot charts if you will, they say, but you will do just as well picking stocks by throwing darts at the stock tables.

As for the news, well, "As the present moves into the future, the stockholders will face all kinds of surprises, but most of the surprises which come this week will not be related, in any systematic manner, to the surprises which will come next week,"[9] writes Paul H. Cootner, who, like many random walkers, is a university professor. So it's almost impossible to predict what the price of a stock will do or to try to beat the market with forecasting tools "because all the information they use is already reflected in stock prices," asserts James H. Lorie, another random walk professor.[10]

This isn't to say that random walk theorists don't think the news has much influence in the market. Professor Fischer Black explains:

> We believe that news has more of an effect on stock prices than fundamental analysts believe. The random walk hypothesis says, in its most complete form, that the news is almost the *only* influence on stock prices, but that it is not at all helpful to an investor who is trying to trade stocks. You can't make money on the news precisely because the market reacts so quickly to all the news. By the time an investor gets a piece of news information about a company, its stock price is likely to have moved already to reflect the new information.

This notion of a market that reacts with the speed of light—too fast for investors to take advantage of any move that might be foretold by the news—is developing into a key element of the random walk theory. Random walkers have decided that their theory works because the stock market is, relatively speaking, a very efficient economic mechanism; if it weren't, investors with inside dope or exceptional savvy would be able to outperform the market consistently—but they don't. Keeping the market efficient are the fundamentalists, technicians, and everybody else who diligently works at trying to fathom the future, acts on his opinions, and advises others to do the same. Thus, for the random walk theory to work, it's important that not very many people believe in it.

But more are. A small but growing number of investment funds are setting up portfolios that take the random walkers' advice and simply try to match the market's performance (as measured by various indices) instead of outdo it. The result is an investment policy that Grandpa would have felt comfortable with —buy and hold. No hopping from one go-go stock to another; instead, develop a diversified portfolio of acceptable risk and volatility and sit on it, come good news or bad.

Random walk clearly is not for gunslingers.

The Contrary Opinion Theory

A contrarian is one who takes a professionally skeptical view of both fundamentalists and technicians. These two schools habitually talk themselves into severe cases of tunnel vision, contrarians argue, and they miss important turns in the market. So, if the fundamentalists are bullish, the contrarian hunts for bearish technical indicators; if the technicians are gloomy, he sifts the fundamental factors for glimmers of sunshine. If, by any chance, the fundamentalists and technicians are in agreement, the contrarian executes an abrupt about-face and marches off the other way.

Here's an example of contrarianism, taken from Alan Abelson's column of April 30, 1973, in *Barron's:* "How far down the drain things will go is strictly anyone's guess. Right now, it all looks pervasively grim. And that's the only hopeful sign on the current market scene."

Contrarians do not always buck the majority, for the majority sometimes is right. Nor is a contrarian necessarily a pessimist; when a bear market has sagged to its bottom, the contrarian frequently is the first to adopt a bullish swagger. Rather, the contrarian evaluates the psychology of the market and then puts his money on the enduring fallibility of humanity.

Contrarian Bradbury K. Thurlow wrote,

It would be pleasant to believe that, in this enlightened age of

computerized decisions, institutional leadership, and broad dissemi-
nation of information, the old boom-and-bust cycle was a thing of the
past. All the evidence, however, appears to point in the opposite direction. The human animal, as a member of a crowd, is still primarily
motivated by the emotions of greed and fear, which still succeed each
other in the market place with sufficient frequency to make the pattern worth studying.[11]

"A crowd," Mr. Thurlow went on, "is gullible, emotional,
unthinking, acutely sensitive to suggestion, unpredictable, impul-
sive and irresistible. A crowd can consist of two or three normally
shrewd businessmen suddenly waxing enthusiastic over the
luncheon table or of millions of people reacting in horror to the
assassination of a President." It is a contrarian tenet that the
heights of speculative mania and the depths of investor depression
are themselves signals of a shift in market direction.

Not surprisingly, contrarians often have a convoluted view of
the news. In Mr. Thurlow's opinion, for example,

Economic forecasts, particularly of the more popular variety
emphasized in the columns of daily newspapers, have a built-in
inertia. That is, they tend to justify the *status quo ante* and equate
themselves with the recent or current state of the stock market. Thus,
characteristically, economic forecasts tend to be most outspokenly optimistic in the late stages of a market rise and the early stages of a
decline and most pessimistic a few months before and after a major
low is reached. Recognized as such, they can be a valuable tool in
forming a composite stock market judgment.[12]

To put it another way, contrarians think good news is good
news unless everybody thinks it's *really* good news, in which case it
might be bad news. It's a Mad Hatter's perspective, to be sure, but
it sometimes makes sense in the stock market wonderland.

Summary and Conclusions

There is more of everything in the stock market these days—
more stocks, more stockholders, more institutional trading, and
more research—and these trends are expected to continue into the
foreseeable future. The competition for stock market profits has

intensified, and so have investors' appetites for the news. We and other observers believe that the result of all this is that the market is more sensitive to the news than it used to be.

How stocks react to news is shaped in part by investors' ideas about how the market works. Many theories have been advanced to explain market movements. Some of these theories downgrade the news as a market-moving factor, but most don't. Followers of the dominant school—the fundamentalists—believe that stock prices reflect developments in the real world, as measured against expectations. Both the expectations and the developments can be discerned by close attention to the news media.

Notes

1. "Are the Institutions Wrecking Wall Street?" *Business Week,* June 2, 1973, p. 58.
2. George J. W. Goodman, " 'Performance' Is the New Name of the Game," in *The Anatomy of Wall Street,* ed. Charles J. Rolo and George J. Nelson (Lippincott, 1968), p. 54.
3. "Are the Institutions Wrecking Wall Street?" p. 59.
4. Ibid., p. 60.
5. Daniel Jay Baum and Ned B. Stiles, *The Silent Partners* (Syracuse University Press, 1965), p. 159.
6. Alan Abelson, "Up and Down Wall Street," *Barron's,* February 19, 1973, p. 1.
7. Herbert Liesner in *Orline D. Foster's Ticker Technique,* ed. Robert H. Persons, Jr. (Investors' Press, 1965), p. 57.
8. Ralph A. Rotnem, "The Valuation of Common Stocks: The Fundamentalist's Approach," in *The Anatomy of Wall Street,* p. 155.
9. Paul H. Cootner, "Random vs. Systematic Changes," in *The Random Character of Stock Market Prices,* ed. Paul H. Cootner (M.I.T. Press, 1964), p. 233.
10. Jonathan R. Laing, "Bye-Bye, Go-Go," *Wall Street Journal,* June 7, 1973, p. 1.

11. Bradbury K. Thurlow, "Contrary Opinion Theory," in *The Anatomy of Wall Street,* p. 182.
12. Ibid., p. 189.

2

The News: Where to Find It

Keeping well informed is easier said than done because probably more is written in the United States about business and the stock market than any other subjects. Daily newspapers, general-interest magazines, and radio and television all give them at least passing attention. There is even a large and growing business press consisting of newspapers, magazines, newsletters, and books. The research departments of stock brokerage firms and investment advisory services crank out company and industry analyses in a volume that might well surpass that of what is usually thought of as the press. The federal government is the world's largest collector and publisher of economic statistics, and universities and private firms also get into this act.

In addition, a sizable portion of the broader flow of news, as reported in the general press, can have a strong bearing on stocks in both general and specific ways. From abroad come stories of war and peace, political turmoil, and the shifting relationships between nations, all of which can affect a U.S. corporate system that is becoming increasingly multinational.

From Washington come stories on the actions of the president, the Congress, the courts, and the regulatory agencies; these become ever more vital to stock market movements as the affairs of private enterprise become more and more of a public concern.

Coverage of state and local governments cannot be ignored. State laws, for example, often are forerunners of national trends—witness California's leadership in setting tougher auto pollution standards in the early 1970s and Massachusetts' impact on the insurance industry, with its adoption of no-fault auto insurance. Similarly, the decisions of municipal governmental bodies in granting cable television franchises will largely determine the fate of that fledgling industry.

Even the sports pages can be read with profit, as more companies try to satisfy the public's growing appetite for all forms of recreation.

In brief, more is written and broadcast about subjects affecting American business than anyone can hope to absorb, so it is useful to narrow the field by eliminating certain media from close consideration. Fortunately this can be done rather easily, particularly when you're concerned with news that has the most direct effect on stocks.

The first large area that can be safely eliminated is broadcasting—radio and television. Many radio and television stations include stock market reports in their periodic news shows, but few of them pay deep attention to the business scene. The main reason for this is that business news rarely is dramatic or, in the case of television, photogenic enough to fit the news format of broadcasters.* Business stories almost invariably contain some statistics, which do not read well over the air. In addition, the great bulk of significant business activity is carried on behind closed doors, where broadcasters' cameras and microphones cannot go. The aspects of the business scene that are open to public view are either mundane (retail sales, building construction) or ceremonial

---

*This probably also accounts for the dearth of novels and motion pictures that have business as a theme.

(supermarket ribbon-cuttings, corporate annual meetings). The broadcasting media have shown little inclination to attempt to overcome these limitations.

The other major segment of the news media that rarely makes itself felt in the stock market is, perhaps surprisingly, the business sections of local daily newspapers. A few daily papers devote substantial resources to business coverage (to attempt to list them would risk excluding some of the deserving), and many others employ individual business reporters and editors who are able and conscientious. But by and large, business news ranks well down on the list of most publishers' priorities. This is apparent from the placement of the business section in most papers—near the back, behind the sports section, and just in front of the want ads—and from the placement of the business news department in most newspaper city rooms—off in a corner somewhere.

The amount of space devoted to business in the average local paper is correspondingly slim. A survey of daily newspapers by a private research firm for the New York and American stock exchanges in 1972 showed that 47% of the business sections of 146 U.S. dailies was occupied by tabular material, such as stock and commodity price listings, and another 29% was devoted to advertising, leaving a bare 24% for editorial matter, including photographs.[1]

Most of this editorial copy usually comes from outside the paper's resident staff. The typical fare consists of a wire service story on the day's stock market activity, a syndicated investment-advice column, a series of one-paragraph items on the day's important business and economic developments (also from a wire service), and, perhaps, an original column or feature on an aspect of the local business scene. Companies outside the paper's circulation area rarely receive any extensive coverage.

Besides skimping on space for business news, most American dailies do not approach the subject with the same diligence that they apply to other fields they cover. This stems in part from the fact that newspapers, too, are businesses, run to show a profit, and most of their revenues come from other businesses in the form of advertising. The practice is rarely stated bluntly as a matter of policy, but newspapers have shown a marked disinclination to bite the hands that feed them by running stories that portray business and businessmen in an unfavorable light. The same can be said for broadcasters, and for the same reasons.

This double standard quickly becomes apparent to the more ambitious young men and women who enter journalism, and they typically respond by shying away from the business page, leaving it to their less energetic and more malleable colleagues. This further works against any incisive coverage of the field.

The upshot for readers is a bias toward the local and the up-beat on the business pages of most papers. Again, there are notable exceptions, but the front pages of the average metropolitan daily usually are more valuable to investors than the pages ostensibly written for their special use.

Any discussion of news media that *are* pertinent to stock price movements must begin with the publications of Dow Jones & Co., the New York-based concern that puts out, among other things, the *Wall Street Journal, Dow Jones News Service,* and *Barron's National Business and Financial Weekly.*

Dow Jones' beginnings were humble indeed. In 1882 three newsmen, Charles H. Dow, Edward D. Jones and a man they hired, set up shop on Wall Street to distribute to clients periodic news bulletins they wrote out in longhand on sheets of tissue paper. Seven years later they got hold of a printing press and started the *Wall Street Journal.* It was anything but an instant success. For approximately the first five decades, the *Journal* was a competent but stodgy business daily whose influence barely extended beyond downtown Manhattan. Its circulation reached about 50,000 in the late 1920s, sank to less than 30,000 in the depressed 1930s, and emerged from World War II at about 75,000.

At that time, however, the paper began broadening its field of interest, brightening its writing style, and just as importantly, expanding its geographic scope with more domestic and foreign news bureaus and a network of regional publishing plants around the country that enabled it to reach most subscribers within a day.

At this writing, it is the only national daily newspaper in the United States.

By the end of 1972, the *Journal's* circulation stood at more than 1,250,000, making it the nation's second largest daily, surpassed only by the tabloid *New York Daily News.* Its subscribers included a good number of corporation presidents, just about the entire membership of the stock brokerage industry, and numerous other influentials.

Dow Jones' president, William F. Kerby, was moved to tell a 1971 gathering of the paper's top editors that "today, without question, the *Wall Street Journal* is the most powerful publication in the world." [2] That is debatable, but the *Journal* is certainly the most powerful and comprehensive publication in the financial field. Horseplayers dream of waking up to find the next day's *Daily Racing Form* on their doorsteps; the *Wall Street Journal* figures similarly in the reveries of stock market investors.

Dow Jones' News Service, commonly called the "ticker" or the "broad tape," is a financial wire service with an estimated 3,500 to 4,000 outlets. Most of its customers are brokerage firms, but it also goes into banks and other financial institutions; daily newspapers, which use it in the same way that they use the more general Associated Press and United Press International wires; and various hotels, resorts, and restaurants where businessmen congregate. It is in operation from early morning until late afternoon each day the stock markets are open, spewing out a constant stream of business news and stock market reports. Many of the stories that appear in the next day's *Wall Street Journal* appear first on the ticker, usually in abbreviated form, although some stories that make the ticker don't make the paper and vice versa. For example, the *Journal's* front page features and columns and its editorial page material never run on the previous day's ticker. Thus, during the business day, the news tends to radiate outward from the brokerage houses.

Barron's, named for Clarence W. Barron, a former owner of Dow Jones whose heirs still are the company's dominant stockholders, is a weekly with a circulation of about 200,000. Its specialties are stock market commentary (often acerbic) and lengthy features about the performance and prospects of industries and individual companies. In the latter regard, it tends to focus on corporations with relatively low price-earnings ratios whose fortunes appear to be taking a turn for the better. Unlike the *Journal*, which frequently diverts its readers with stories about subjects that are off the financial track, *Barron's* sticks strictly to business. It recently has begun broadening its coverage to include other forms of investment, but it is still written expressly for the stock market devotee.

Dow Jones does not have business publishing all to itself by any means. Until 1968, it did have a virtual monopoly as a U.S. financial wire service, but this was ended in January of that year by Reuters Ltd., the venerable London-based news agency with correspondents around the world. Reuters' invasion of Dow Jones' ticker territory followed by several months a move by Dow Jones, in partnership with the Associated Press, to sell a business wire service to financial institutions in Europe, which had been Reuters' turf.

As of 1972, Reuters' share of the U.S. ticker market was placed at between 5% (Dow Jones' estimate) and 20% (Reuters' estimate). Neutral observers put the actual percentage somewhere in between. The competition between the two agencies, however, was quite real. Dow Jones' U.S. reporting staff of some 150 was several times larger than Reuters', and it was first to carry most items of business news; but Reuters, stronger abroad, scored numerous market-moving beats and said it was in the field to stay.

The mere fact of competition in the business news wire field altered the content of the medium. When Reuters came on the U.S. scene with modern, high-speed transmission equipment, Dow Jones was pushed to respond at considerable expense by installing faster machines of its own. This has vastly increased the amount of business news that the brokers et al. receive during the business day. Both agencies carry reports on the activities of over-the-counter companies that Dow Jones considered too small to bother with when it had the monopoly. This development has coincided with the increase in trading volume of over-the-counter issues.

Also, corporate public relations men found that the presence of Reuters gave them a kind of leverage with the Dow Jones' News Service that they formerly lacked. "Some PR men, in calling in a release to DJ, will mention that the news also is being called to Reuters. This, if handled properly, can serve to give DJ an extra prod to act quickly," one public relations newsletter reported. The letter advised its readers to "milk the Reuters-Dow Jones compeition for whatever it's worth."[3] Experience indicates that the advice has been widely followed.

The other main area of competition in the publication of business and financial news is the magazine field. Dominant among the weeklies is *Business Week*, a publication of McGraw-Hill Inc. *Business Week*, whose circulation at the end of 1972 stood at 726,000, broadly covers the business scene. It maintains news bureaus in most major American cities and has more foreign news offices than the *Wall Street Journal*. Indeed, foreign coverage is one of its strong points—no small factor in this era of rapid U.S. business expansion abroad—and it devotes considerable space to Washington news affecting business. Most weeks it pictures a top American business executive on its cover and carries a lengthy story, usually upbeat, inside about the man and his company.

Forbes, a semimonthly with a 1972 circulation of 628,000, concentrates on stories about companies in transition. It carries stock market commentary by brokerage house analysts who have a wide range of viewpoints, and annually rates the performance of more than 500 common stock mutual funds.

The leader among the monthlies is *Fortune*, (1972 circulation 584,000), published by Time Inc. Handsomely illustrated and smoothly written, it takes a longer view of things than do the weeklies, covering fewer subjects more thoroughly and looking further into the future (too far, according to some critics). However, some of its most notable efforts are detailed reconstructions of how large and apparently imposing companies went wrong.

Dun's Review, another monthly (circulation 203,000),

addresses itself mainly to spotting new trends and techniques in management. It, too, carries regular columns on stock market trends.

The major general-interest magazines—*Time* and *Newsweek* —have stepped up their coverage of business and the economy in recent years. *Time* has done this primarily by expanding the attention it gives to economic news; *Newsweek* has added a "Wall Street" column by veteran-business-writer Clem Morgello and has signed on several well-known economists to give their viewpoints periodically. The impact of both these magazines on individual stocks can be great because of their large circulations (*Time*'s was about 4.3 million at the end of 1972; *Newsweek*'s was 2.7 million) and because they reach many readers who do not read the specialized business press.

Consumer Reports, the monthly publication of the nonprofit Consumers Union of the United States, a consumer protection group, has become increasingly pointed in its criticisms of products and the companies that make them, and its stock market impact has grown accordingly. Its June 1971 attack on the effectiveness of the motor oil additive made by STP Corp., for instance, triggered a one-day drop in the price of STP stock of $14 to $39 a share.

Even publications that rarely pay attention to business can shake individual stocks. A case in point was the August 1972 issue of *Saga* magazine. *Saga* usually aims at hairy-chested types with spreads on adventure, sports, and pretty girls; but that issue included an article titled "Wreckreational Vehicles—Deathtraps on Wheels," which sent the stocks of Winnebago Industries and other makers of motor homes into a tailspin. We will take a closer look at this situation later.

There is, of course, more—much more. Just about every industry has at least one trade newspaper or magazine devoted exclusively to its activities, and some, such as the steel, auto, and chemical industries, have more. Upward of 5,000 newsletters are published annually[4] in the United States, most of them promising "inside" information or analysis that isn't available elsewhere.

Such publications often provide valuable information to students of particular industries, but they generally have small circulations and thus don't affect stocks unless their articles are picked up by the broader press.

The types of publications mentioned above are a diverse lot, but they share in common the presumption that they have no direct monetary stake in the activities they write about; when they speak well or ill of an enterprise, and, thus, its stock, it is seen as a service to their readers rather than a promotion of their own financial interests.* Indeed, it is from this disinterested posture that the constituents of the American press derive much of their authority and credibility.

There is, however, an increasingly important source of stock market information and commentary that operates from a quite different set of standards—the research arms of the nation's broker-dealer firms. For them, analysis of stock market values has become a vital part of their primary business of buying and selling securities on behalf of their customers. Financial articles in the broader press usually just set down the facts about a company as the writer sees them and leaves any trading conclusions to the reader. The published reports of the broker-dealer firms usually end with a recommendation to buy, sell, or hold the stock of the company in question.

In the previous chapter, we noted how the research output of the brokerage houses provides a context in which news about a company can be evaluated, but it also can serve as a primary source of stock market information. The extent to which brokers have become part of the financial press is illustrated by the fairly typical example of Shearson-Hammill Inc., a large New York-based firm, which in 1972 had some 60 domestic sales offices and four more abroad. In that year, Shearson-Hammill employed 30

*This presumption isn't always true. In 1957 the business editor of *Time* was fired after the SEC charged that he bought and sold stocks in companies about which his magazine was planning articles. In 1972, the SEC obtained an injunction barring similar manipulations by a financial columnist for the *Los Angeles Herald-Examiner* and his son, who edited a West Coast business monthly.

analysts, about double the number of 10 years before, and two full-time editors to process their reports. The company maintained its own printing facility in New York.

Shearson-Hammill analysts produced periodic reports on almost 200 companies, including about 90 on its regular recommended list, 40 in which it made an over-the-counter market, and 60 or so more in which a sizable number of its 100,000 customers were interested. The reports took two forms—lengthy and detailed ones for institutional clients and briefer ones for individual, or retail, accounts. This was a common practice in the industry and stemmed from the express wishes of the two classes of customers. The reports were wired or mailed to the firm's 1,100 salesmen, who forwarded them to customers. Press runs ranged as high as 10,000 copies.

In addition, Shearson-Hammill published a weekly investment policy letter for distribution to salesmen and, hence, to customers. Running 600 to 700 words, the letter included commentary on the general market and advice on investment strategy. Monthly statements to customers included a 2,500-word report titled "Business & Securities," which delved into those subjects in greater detail.

In all, Shearson-Hammill turned its printing presses several million times in 1972, more times than all but a handful of members of what is more commonly thought of as the business press.

Because of the close connection between the selling and research ends of the brokerage business, the vast majority of stock trading recommendations that come out of the brokerage firms are buys rather than sells or holds, and what sells do emerge usually are imparted privately to owners of the stocks rather than broadcast widely. Buys, of course, are of potential use to virtually all of a broker's clientele, while only owners can sell; but brokers also hesitate to recommend sells for fear of incurring the wrath of the companies involved. This could be held against them if they bid to manage the equity or debt offerings of the concerns in question. The vast preponderance of buy over sell advice at large in the marketplace is believed to impart an upward bias to stocks generally.

The security analysts, who are responsible for the recommendations brokers turn out, come from a wide variety of backgrounds. Most have some formal training in business subjects, of course, but the profession has no formal entrance requirements or standard academic discipline. A look at the field by the *Wall Street Journal* several years ago turned up a geologist, a lawyer, several writers, a former stenographer and a former best-selling song writer, among others.[5] Judgment and intuition are highly prized.

The Financial Analysts Federation has made an effort to upgrade professional standards with its Chartered Financial Analysts program, begun in the early 1960s and administered by the University of Virginia. To secure a CFA certificate, an analyst must meet various experience requirements and pass examinations in accounting, economics, techniques of analysis, and portfolio management. As of early 1972, some 3,200 charters had been issued, covering roughly 20% of the profession. However, few of the brokerage houses, banks, mutual funds, insurance companies, and investment counselors who employ analysts have made the degree a condition of employment or promotion.

The quality of the advice that brokers make available to the public, likewise, varies widely. The SEC, in its 1963 study of the securities markets, reported finding "no general correlation between the size of a brokerage firm and the size and quality of its research staff."[6] This conclusion was supported in detail by R. E. Diefenbach, vice-president and director of research for United States & Foreign Securities Corp., a mutual fund, in an article published in the January-February 1972 issue of *Financial Analysts Journal*.

Mr. Diefenbach took note of all the buy and sell recommendations his fund received from brokerage houses between November 17, 1967 and May 23, 1969, charted the stocks' progress for the year that followed the reports and compared them with the performance of Standard & Poor's 425-stock industrial average. Of

1,209 buy recommendations from 24 firms that passed his desk in that period, only 47% outperformed the broad-based index. In total, the recommendations of 12 of the firms did better than the index, while those of the other 12 did worse.

"There would certainly seem to be little to choose between this group of recommendations and a random selection process," Mr. Diefenbach wrote. "Sources providing large numbers of recommendations do not seem to have done either significantly better or worse than those producing fewer."

Mr. Diefenbach related that he received just 46 sell recommendations in his period of study, a statistic that is remarkable in itself because in its later stage the market headed into its most severe decline in more than 30 years. He found that on the whole the sell advice was well taken; the stocks in question did do poorly. But he concluded, "We were unable *anywhere* to find that quality of excellence so often claimed for institutional research . . . [it was] consistently mediocre."

Despite such findings, though, the analysts do move the market. Wall Streeters agree that brokerage house reports provide the dominant rationale for the stock trading decisions of both institutional and individual investors. One needn't be on every broker's mailing list to become aware of key reports; they are increasingly finding their way into the news columns of the broader press, and more and more analysts—in addition to doing their regular chores—are becoming columnists for business publications.

The combination of a strongly worded analyst's report and its coverage in a large-circulation newspaper or magazine can shake stocks more than either could alone. An example of this came in November 1972, when reports became widespread that Oppenheimer & Co., a New York-based firm with a large institutional following, was preparing to release a study casting doubt on the long-term prospects of the then fast-growing hospital management field. In little over a week's time, the stocks of two major companies in the business dropped by around 20% on *rumors* of the study. The day its existence was confirmed in the *Wall Street Journal*'s widely read "Heard on the Street" column,[7] they dived again. One of the issues took a single-day drubbing of 13%.

Summary and Conclusions

The impossibility of reading everything that might bear on your investments requires that some corners be cut. Those whose business it is to follow the securities markets closely say that the most important element in any reading program is balance. Some source of reliable daily financial news—either the *Wall Street Journal* or the financial pages of a metropolitan newspaper that takes business news seriously—is considered a must. So is a large daily dose of national and international news. A proper reading list might also include a weekly newsmagazine, a business periodical or two, and the regular mailings of a brokerage house.

Market-affecting news can be carried first in almost any publication, but truly important stories always manage to find their way quickly into broader circulation (editors, too, can read). The same can be said about security analysts' views on widely held stocks, especially if the views run against the current consensus. Despite the widely documented record of their fallibility, publications increasingly are quoting analysts as experts or signing them on as columnists.

Wall Streeters agree, albeit reluctantly, that nothing much stays secret long these days.

Notes

1. *A Survey of Business/Financial Sections of Daily Newspapers,* Total Research Inc., for the American Stock Exchange and the New York Stock Exchange, 1972.
2. Carol J. Loomis, "One Story the *Wall Street Journal* Won't Print," *Fortune,* August, 1971, p. 140.
3. "How to Play Reuters Against Dow Jones," *The Corporate Communications Report* (newsletter), August–September, 1972, p. 2.

4. Business Bulletin, *Wall Street Journal,* October 5, 1972, p. 1.
5. Frederick C. Klein, "Students of Stocks," *Wall Street Journal,* January 23, 1968, p. 1.
6. *Special Study of Security Markets of the Securities and Exchange Commission, Part 1,* U.S. Government Printing Office (Washington, D.C., 1963), p. 144.
7. Dan Dorfman, "Heard on the Street," *Wall Street Journal,* November 27, 1972, p. 33.

3

The News: Where It Comes From

Most of the news that fills the nation's business publications—and serves as the raw material from which security analysts draw their judgements—comes directly from the companies involved. Publicly owned corporations are required by the Securities & Exchange Commission to disseminate as quickly as possible any information that can have a material effect on their operations or prospects. These standards are echoed by the rules of the New York and American stock exchanges and by the National Association of Securities Dealers, which oversees the national over-the-counter market.

A whole profession—public relations—has grown up around the need for companies to inform their shareholders and the investing public at large about their activities. Just about every publicly owned corporation employs PR men or contracts with an outside agency to perform this service. Aside from their common function of lily gilding, the role of public relations men or women varies widely from company to company. It is our observation, however, that the information policies of most companies are established by top management and that any credit or blame that derives from those policies should go to that level rather than to the PR functionaries who carry out management's wishes.

Items that demand prompt disclosure include annual and quarterly reports of sales and earnings, the declaration or omission of cash dividends, stock splits and stock dividends, mergers and acquisitions, significant new products or discoveries, changes in top management or ownership control, legal actions taken by or against a company, tender offers for the shares of other firms, major changes in capital spending plans, strikes and new labor contracts covering unionized employees, important private borrowings, and the intention to make new equity or debt offerings to the public.

This list has been growing in recent years and is likely to continue to grow as the SEC and other regulatory agencies press for ever more complete disclosures aimed at giving investors more on which to base their decisions and protecting them from being victimized by corporate insiders who possess special information by virtue of their involvement in company affairs. At this writing, moves are afoot to require companies to issue periodic earnings forecasts; reveal more about their depreciation, pension-funding, and taxpaying practices; and spell out more quickly incipient problems that could have a negative effect on future earnings.

So stated, a corporation's disclosure responsibilities appear to be clear-cut and subject to easy, mechanical interpretations, but in practice this is far from true. Definitions of who must reveal what, to whom, and when, have been laboriously established by the SEC, the stock exchanges, and the courts, often on a case-by-case basis. While the trend toward greater disclosure is clear, it hasn't been smooth.

Indeed, the entire subject of disclosure has long been a bone of contention between companies and the agencies established to protect investors. Generally, companies have resisted attempts to make them tell more, arguing that the cost of accumulating the necessary data is burdensome, that its release unfairly aids competitors and labor unions with which they must bargain, and that unless an investor is an expert in their lines of business, he can't evaluate the data properly.

At the turn of the twentieth century, very few publicly owned companies issued annual reports or held open shareholders' meetings. As recently as 1926, a census by the New York Stock Exchange showed that only 339 of its 957 listed firms issued annual reports, and just 242 produced quarterly income statements.[1] Corporate financial reporting on a broad scale didn't occur until the public uproar following the stock market crash of 1929 forced the passage of the Federal Securities Act of 1933 and the Securities and Exchange Act of 1934.

Even today, when the large majority of companies are living up to the letter of disclosure rules, compliance often isn't wholehearted. Surenda Singhvi, professor of finance at Miami University and a close student of corporate disclosure practices, wrote: "When left to their own initiative, corporate managements [have shown] little desire to provide full and fair information to their stockholders."[2]

The willingness of companies to discuss their affairs varies with their condition. Most American business executives do not subscribe to the Oriental belief that one should not tempt the gods by crowing about one's success; they are most forthcoming when things are good and tend to keep quiet when things turn bad.

Thus, sophisticated investors assume that when a company volunteers to talk about itself, the news must be favorable. *Barron's* documented this assumption some years ago by charting the stock price movements of the 129 companies that made presentations at the lunchtime meetings of the New York Society of Security Analysts, the nation's largest analysts' group, over a 6½-month period. Appearances before analysts' groups are voluntary and usually are announced in advance by the companies and societies involved.

Barron's found that the stock of 72 of the 129 concerns that spoke to the New York analysts outperformed the Dow Jones Industrial Average in the two weeks *before* their appearances, while the stocks of just 20 of the 129 did better than the DJIA in the weeks immediately *after* their talks. In almost half of the cases in which a substantial price rise took place prior to a company's appearance, a sell-off occurred the day of the talk or the next day.[3] Apparently, the mere fact that a company volunteered to discuss itself was better news than what it actually said.

Similarly, good news tends to be reported quickly to the public and bad news slowly. Victor Niederhoffer and Patrick J. Regan of the University of California looked at the 50 best performers on the New York Stock Exchange in 1970 and the 50 worst, and found that 88% of the top 50 companies reported their fiscal year earnings within two months of its conclusion, compared to just 40% of the bottom 50 companies. Four of the five firms that took more than three months to report showed losses.[4]

When they must reveal unpleasant information to the public, corporations try to cast it in the best possible light. If profits are down and sales are up, sales will get the featured treatment. If both are down, something in the future usually looks promising enough to warrant prominent comment.

Especially unhappy news is frequently tucked away where it might escape notice. For instance, the quarterly earnings report of one small midwestern company proudly announced a sales increase and said that earnings "dipped" because of a "temporary decline in orders" for one of its major products. Far down in the release, the company revealed that orders for the product declined because the assembly line for the product had to be shut down for most of the quarter to correct quality control problems. The implication that orders may have been lost permanently due to the shutdown was left unsaid. Such practices, which aren't infrequent, might comply with the letter of disclosure law, but the responsibility shifts to the press to present a correct picture of a company's operations.*

---

*Sometimes companies don't bother to report bad news at all. Some years ago the *Wall Street Journal*'s Pittsburgh bureau learned of a sizable layoff at Westinghouse Electric Co. through a postcard from a laid-off worker. Competitors, suppliers, union officials, and disgruntled former executives have been prime sources for stories about companies that didn't choose to discuss their own problems.

The most important type of news that companies report is their profit as expressed in earnings per share of common stock outstanding. Earnings-per-share has long played a vital role in setting stock prices, but its importance has been changed and magnified as more investors enter the market in search of capital appreciation instead of dividend income. In recent years, the price-earnings ratio of a company's stock (calculated by dividing the current stock price by per-share earnings in the most recent fiscal year) has emerged as the key measure by which Wall Street evaluates a company's performance. In September 1972, the Associated Press, which supplies the stock price tables that most newspapers carry, began including price-earnings multiples for every company in its New York and American stock exchange listings. This not only recognizes the measure's importance, but it also focuses even more attention on it.

Whether a stock is selling at a "proper" price-earnings multiple is one of the enduring mysteries of Wall Street. Analysts have come up with various formulas to determine this; usually, they take into account the company's historical earnings record and the P/E multiples for its industry and the market as a whole. While the exact mix hasn't been established to anyone's complete satisfaction, the factor of steady earnings growth is generally judged to predominate. "The farther out into the future you can see earnings growth, the higher multiple you are willing to pay for this year's earnings," summarized Stephen Albert of the brokerage firm of G. H. Walker & Co.[5]

As that statement indicates, a company's annual and quarterly earnings reports can't be properly evaluated unless one also knows what that company is *expected* to earn. This leads to the subject of earnings forecasting. Analysts typically, but not always, make earnings projections after talking to the company officers. Their profits estimates for large concerns, a crucial part of their recommendations of trading action, are published weekly in *Standard & Poor's Earnings Forecaster.*

Company executives also forecast their firms' future profits directly for the business press, and the practice is becoming more widespread. Dow Jones' News Service daily carries numerous interviews with top officials on their companies' outlooks, and earnings projections almost always play the featured role. Reuters also runs such interviews, although less often than Dow Jones.

Studies have shown that analysts' profit forecasts like their advice on the buying and selling of stocks, often leave something to be desired. Martin E. Zweig, assistant professor of economics and finance at City University of New York, took note of two such studies in a *Barron's* article and reported that in both simply projecting a company's recent past earnings pattern into the next year turned out just as accurately as the projections of professional seers, who presumably used more complicated methods.[6] Other studies showed that company executives could forecast their own firms' future profits only slightly better than could "naive" models and that they sometimes missed the mark widely, Professor Zweig reported.

Wall Street, however, still treats earnings projections with the greatest respect. In their comparison of the 50 best and 50 worst New York Stock Exchange performers of 1970, Niederhoffer and Regan found that the ·big gainers consistently reported higher earnings than had been estimated, while *all* of the big losers on which profits had been predicted actually did much worse. One must conclude that the stock-price records of both groups stemmed more from comparisons of their earnings performance with expectations than with any absolute standards.

Companies, of course, are required to release more than just sales and earnings figures to the public. Their annual reports (but not their quarterly ones) must contain balance sheet listings of such assets as cash, accounts receivable and the value of inventories, plant, and equipment, and liabilities, such as outstanding debts and accounts payable. Nevertheless, Wall Street's emphasis on profit has turned attention away from the balance sheet in recent years, and this has been reflected in the press. The *Wall Street Journal* used to run selected balance sheet items of large companies but discontinued the practice a half-dozen years ago because of lack of space and reader interest.

Many observers believe that both ·the press and investors

ought to look more closely at corporate balance sheets. The 1970 financial collapse of the giant Penn Central Railroad took Wall Street pretty much by surprise, but it shouldn't have, according to Paul E. Dascher, an accounting professor at Virginia Polytechnic Institute. He looked up the Penn Central's 1969 balance sheet, computed some of the assets-to-liabilities ratios that are thought to be crucial indicators of a company's financial health, and compared them with those of the nation's nine next-largest railroads. Penn Central figures lagged well behind the other railroads in many key areas, including cash flow to total debt, total debt to total assets, and current assets to current debt. He concluded, "If existing techniques for detecting financial weakness had been applied to the published financial data for the Penn Central, they would have predicted failure."[7]

Much the same thing can be said about examining the prospectuses companies must issue when they want to sell securities to the public. In many ways, these are the most revealing reports companies publish. Editors of the *Wall Street Journal,* in a memorandum urging reporters to pay closer attention to prospectuses, noted that some keen-eyed members of the paper's staff found the following nuggets in such documents: A major oil company's plan to sell or close a large number of its retail outlets; a big expense write-off by a major airline; and the fact that a company president's brother, who previously had been a trumpet player, had been named to manage one of the concern's plants. None of these items had been previously announced.

Most other kinds of news that emanate from corporate headquarters present fewer problems of discovery and interpretation. Stock dividends and splits usually are greeted favorably by investors, although there is no intrinsic reason why one share of stock worth $50 should be more valuable than two worth $25 each. Mergers and acquisitions also are usually well received, at least initially. Principals in such transactions invariably forecast various advantages, and their statements are duly quoted in the press, but it usually takes a while to determine if the advertised benefits will materialize.

Price increases, sometimes announced and sometimes not, are good for the companies that get them and bad for ones that must pay, although the latter usually find ways to pass them on to their own customers.

The aspect of corporate life that is perhaps best shielded from public view is the jockeying among executives for top positions, even though such information can bear importantly on a company's prospects. Just about every business publication carries stories about changes in management of large companies, but these tend to be as bloodless as the news releases that announce them. Executives rarely are portrayed as being fired, kicked up-stairs, or elbowed aside; they "resign to pursue other activities" or are "named to the newly created post of vice-chairman" or some such.

The reasons for this are several. One is that executive in-fighting is almost universal, and publications cannot spare the time to investigate all of it. Also, the losers in executive-suite struggles—the best sources for such stories—usually aren't anxious to discuss their personal failures.

Mostly, though, companies don't talk about this because they don't have to. There is no SEC rule that a corporation reveal that its chairman and its president don't get along, or that one vice-president is more likely to succeed than another because he's a better tennis player, and it's not likely there ever will be.

From Washington

Right behind corporations as a source of news affecting busi-ness is the federal government apparatus in Washington. To at-tempt to list all the ways that the actions of the government can make themselves felt in the stock market is beyond the scope of this book, so a brief outline must suffice.

The major way that the president and Congress affect business is through their taxing and spending powers. The annual federal budget is the nation's most important financial document, spelling out national priorities for the fiscal year ahead. It is closely studied by economists for clues to both the direction of the general economy and the specific areas that might advance or decline. How much money is allocated for defense, education, road building, mass transportation, atomic energy development, and the multitude of other governmental concerns has the most direct bearing on companies involved in such endeavors.

The prospects of many companies and industries are vitally affected by news from the federal regulatory agencies. Railroads can't raise their interstate rates or alter their routes without approval from the Interstate Commerce Commission; airlines can't take similar actions unless the Civil Aeronautics Board approves; the Federal Communications Commission holds sway over telephone and telegraph companies and broadcasters. The list goes on.

Correct anticipation and interpretation of agency decisions can provide the best sort of clues to significant changes in a company's fortunes. An example of this was recounted by Benjamin M. Rosen, research director of Coleman & Co., a New York firm that specializes in stock market research for institutions, in an interview with the *New York Times* that ran on December 4, 1972. Mr. Rosen's buy recommendation on the stock of American Telephone & Telegraph Co. was credited with starting a major upturn in that stock in late 1972.

The *Times* story, in part, went like this:*

Q: If you had to pinpoint it to one thing, when did the light bulb flash in your mind alerting you to the possibilities of AT&T's recovery?

A [Mr. Rosen]: The trigger was in July [1972]. That's when the Federal Communications Commission decided to reopen the critical case involving Telephone's rate of return on its interstate earnings. I thought this development might be favorable for the company, partly because costs had gone up since the recommendation of the FCC hearing examiner back in August of 1971. Also it was most unusual for the FCC to reopen the case. . . .

Q: At the time of your first [August] report, what was your attitude toward the company?

A: We felt the positive factors in the company's outlook more than outweighed the negative ones. . . . Secondly was the FCC

* © 1971/1972 by The New York Times Company. Reprinted by permission.

decision on allowable rate of return, which would demonstrate whether indeed we might look forward to a more favorable regulatory environment. . . .

Q: And what actually happened?

A: The quarterly dividend was raised to 70 cents a share from 65 cents on Aug. 16. The third-quarter earnings of $1.10 a share against 95 cents exceeded our optimistic expectations of $1.06. As for the rate of return, we were exactly on target, luckily enough. The hearing examiner had suggested a target figure of 8.25%. What came out [of the FCC] in November was an allowable range of 8.5% to 9%.[8]

Measured in terms of sheer volume of words and numbers, the federal government makes most of its business news in its capacity as scorekeeper for the U.S. economy. Rarely a day goes by that some governmental department doesn't issue a new measure of economic activity. The prime source of economic statistics is the Commerce Department's Bureau of Economic Analysis, which keeps track of measures of national income, spending, and investment. The Labor Department's Bureau of Labor Statistics charts trends in employment and unemployment. The Census Bureau of the Commerce Department tracks orders and inventories. Again, the list goes on.

Measures of national economic activity usually are released to the press one at a time and, as such, present even sophisticated readers with problems of interpretation. There is a tendency to regard any upward movement of business activity as good news, but this isn't necessarily the case, especially where the stock market is concerned. The most widely used means of attaining a perspective on the flow of economic data is the cyclical indicator approach, which attempts to relate the movement of individual measures of activity to the broader cycles of expansion and contraction that the general economy historically has gone through.

The cyclical indicator approach singles out portions of the economy that have shown a tendency to move differently in relation to business cycles as a whole. Leading indicators are those that usually reach peaks or troughs *before* corresponding turns in aggregate business activity. Roughly coincident indicators tend to move together with the business curve. Lagging indicators usually reach their turning points *after* the general economy turns.

Business Conditions Digest, a monthly publication of the Bureau of Economic Analysis, charts 78 cyclical indicators: 40 leaders, 26 coincident indicators, and 12 laggers. Most closely followed, however, is its short list of 12 leaders, eight roughly coincident indicators, and six laggers. These have been picked because they are "more selective" than the others and are "substantially unduplicated" by other measures, according to *Business Conditions Digest.*

Stock price movements, as measured by Standard & Poor's 500-stock index, is in the short list of economic leaders, which means that stocks tend to turn upward while business in general is in recession and downward before the next recession hits. The other leaders are the average workweek (in hours) of industrial workers; average initial claims for state unemployment insurance (inverted scale); net new-business formations; new orders for durable goods; contracts and orders for plant and equipment; new permits to build private homes; changes in book value of manufacturing and trade inventories; industrial materials prices; corporate after-tax profits; the ratio of price to unit labor costs in manufacturing; and changes in consumer installment debt.

The reasons why most of these measures should lead business cycles are simple. To name a few, orders for durable goods and heavy equipment must precede their manufacture by a good period, and the issuance of building permits must precede construction. Manufacturers lay off workers during a recession and put the remainder of their work force on short hours; when business starts turning upward, full workweeks are restored before those laid off are rehired. Costs tend to be lower and profits higher during turn-around periods than in the later stages of an expansion, when workers are hard to find and marginal equipment must be utilized to increase production. Stock prices, of course, tend to rise with profits.

The eight roughly coincident indicators include the measures that receive the most news attention: gross national product in both current and stable dollars, personal income, industrial production, manufacturing and trade sales, retail sales, nonagricultural employment, and the unemployment rate (inverted scale). When the economy is discussed, it is usually in terms of the coincident indicators.

The six laggers are the percentage of persons unemployed 15 weeks or more, business expenditures for new plant and equipment (more gear is needed as production nears peaks), the book value of manufacturing and trade inventories, commercial and industrial loans outstanding, and bank rates on short-term business loans (money gets tight).

Determining what phase a business cycle is in at a particular time by applying the indicators is a difficult matter. For one thing, collecting and publishing the data takes time, so reported figures generally lag behind the developments they portray. For another, month-by-month reports often are based largely on estimates rather than on actual survey figures, and thus are subject to later revision. The composite index that combines the 12 leading indicators has been particularly susceptible to revision because it is reported monthly, even though data on four of its components (net business formations, inventories, profits, and changes in consumer debt) are collected quarterly.

Finally, there is no intrinsic mechanism in the data that indicates *when* the economy is taking a turn. The indicators do not move together smoothly and their components may take independent turns that do not precede general movements. The stock market in particular has gone off on its own on several occasions; for example, the declines of 1946, 1962, and 1966 weren't followed by a downturn in the general economy or in corporate profits, the factor with which stocks are most closely associated. Conversely, in the 1950–52 period, stocks rose steadily while profits dropped.

Various ways have been tried to jigger the indicators to predict stock market turns, such as splitting the time-series groups into long and short leaders so that changes in the longs (including such laggers as unit labor costs) can point the way toward changes in the short leader of stock prices. These approaches, however, have encountered problems of their own, including the constant one of interpretation.[9]

Some economists have fastened on another government-released statistic—changes in the rate of U.S. monetary growth—as a means of forecasting major stock price moves. Their numbers and the attention they receive in the press have grown with the influence of the monetarist school of economists, led by Professor Milton Friedman of the University of Chicago. This group believes that variation in the money supply, not government taxing and spending policies, is the prime source of the economy's cyclical swings.

Monetarist Beryl W. Sprinkel, senior vice-president and economist at Harris Trust and Savings Bank of Chicago, has related money supply changes to stock market turns and has found that marked downward swings in money growth have preceded bear markets by an average of nine months, while an acceleration of monetary growth has led bull markets by two to three months. He cautions, however, that "the data indicate only the *average* lead of changes in monetary growth prior to a change in stock prices" and says there is "no apparent inherent theoretical reason" why bear-market leads are so much longer than bull-market leads. He adds, "Although averages may be useful statistical summaries for some purposes, they may be misleading in other cases. Well known is the story about the gentleman who drowned in attempting to wade across a river that averaged only one foot deep."[10]

Interest rates are another type of financial statistic that has had an important effect on stocks, especially in recent years. These emanate from both private and governmental sources. The main measure of interest rates in the private sector is the so-called prime rate that banks charge their most credit-worthy commercial customers. Among government agencies, the U.S. Treasury sets interest rates in its periodic public borrowings, and the Federal Reserve Board does it through its widely followed discount.rate, the charge it levies on its loans to member banks.

Rising interest charges are almost always bad for stocks. They make corporate expansion more expensive and thus more difficult, dampen demand for homes, autos and other high-priced consumer durables, and, when translated into higher bond yields, draw money away from common stocks. In later chapters, we will trace the role of interest rates in the major market movements of the 1965–72 period.

Other Sources

News from abroad can affect stocks in both general and specific ways. Flare-ups in major foreign conflicts, such as those between Israel and the Arab states, can have a depressing influence on investor psychology; moves by foreign governments to expropriate American property or raise their share of the fruits thereof are an important element in the evaluation of companies in the oil and mineral extraction fields. The policies of foreign governments on imports and exports can affect a wide variety of U.S. concerns. International monetary fluctuation—and its attendant uncertainty—was a major stock market depressant throughout the troubled early 1970s.

Back on the domestic scene, an investor need not be his own economist to interpret the economy's shifting tides; members of that calling frequently speak to the public through the press. Economic analysis is especially abundant around year-end, when large banks and university business schools assemble panels of economists to give their views on the year ahead. In addition, a number of publications have hired economists as regular contributors. Paul Samuelson, Milton Friedman, and Henry Wallich have served in such capacity at *Newsweek*, giving readers a range of perspectives from which to choose. The stock market impact of this is difficult to measure, but the views of prominent economists certainly help make up the backdrop of expectations against which the market moves.

A number of agencies, private as well as public, poll different groups on their expectations and intentions for future periods. The University of Michigan surveys consumer sentiment quarterly; Dun & Bradstreet surveys businessmen for expected sales, prices, and inventory levels; and the Commerce Department periodically looks at corporate capital spending plans. The limitations of these surveys are inherent in their definitions—people don't always do what they say they will. But these surveys, too, figure into the calculations of stock market decision makers.

Finally, and also importantly, many of the broader business stories that appear in the press originate with the publications themselves, insofar as they initiate the inquiries and draw conclusions from the material they collect. This category isn't a clear one by any means. In their investigations publications may draw on corporate sources, economists, government statistics, security analysts, and other observers. The conclusions, however, may well be the writer's own, and they may or may not coincide with those of the principal actors in the particular drama.

Much of the criticism leveled at the press generally comes as a result of this conclusion-drawing process—of its going "beyond the facts." It must be understood, however, that the American press isn't simply a conduit for official versions of things, be they corporate or governmental, and that the usefulness of a publication to its readers comes largely as a result of its ability to explain and interpret the jumble of facts and feelings that comprise reality. The conclusions stated in a news story aren't necessarily the correct or only ones, but their statement, if backed by conscientious investigation, traditionally has been a legitimate function of the press.

When applied to the stock market, stories that go beyond simple reporting of statements or statistics can have a substantial impact, especially on individual stocks. Unlike corporate earnings releases and the announcement of government economic measures that are fairly well predictable as to time, stories originated by publications usually come as a surprise, fulfilling one of the most often-stated requirements for market-affecting news. Beyond that, the impact of a story varies according to the nature of its conclusions and the reputation of the publication that carries it.

Thus is it that the *Consumer Reports* article casting doubt on the usefulness of STP's oil additive triggered a 26% drop in that company's stock in a single day, or that *Saga's* strongly worded condemnation of the safety of recreational vehicles had a similar effect on a whole industry.

Thus it is, too, that an October 24, 1972, article in the *Wall Street Journal,* based around the less than sensational theme that Gillette Co., the maker of shaving products, was shedding its "stodgy" ways, spurred an increase of that firm's stock price by 10% in a single month. It is the type of story which Wall Street pays attention to.

Summary and Conclusions

Most business news originates with the companies that make it. Companies tell the public what they are up to because they are required by law to do so. Despite corporate resistance, the list of information that companies must report has grown in recent years, and it is likely to continue growing.

Companies generally seek out press attention when things are good and try to avoid it when things are bad. When a company volunteers to talk about itself, it is assumed that it has glad tidings to report. When bad news must be revealed, it usually is done in the least obtrusive way.

The combination of corporate emphasis on the positive and willingness of many publications to go along with it results in a pronounced tilt toward optimism in the business press. Since journalistic enterprise is rarely required to uncover the good that corporations do, stories that periodicals dig up on their own tend to point out problems that haven't been aired before.

The federal government is a major business news maker, both in its activities that affect business directly (taxing, spending, and regulating) and in its capacity as scorekeeper for the American economy. The problem with government statistics isn't any lack of them but rather their interpretation, especially as they relate to stock market trends. Various methods have been tried, but no measure or group of measures of economic activity has been shown to fluctuate consistently so as to predict the ups and downs of stock prices.

Corporate profit forecasts by company executives and security analysts, economists' predictions and surveys of business, and consumer sentiment all help establish the expectations against which actual economic activity is measured. Wall Street pros agree that the prices of individual stocks reflect a relationship between earnings performance and expectations rather than objective standards.

National and international news that isn't directly about business is important to stocks mainly insofar as it affects the national "mood." A recent vivid example was the 1973 Senate inquiry into the Watergate scandal, which coincided with a broad-based market decline. It might not have *caused* the downturn, but it certainly helped.

Notes

1. Surenda Singhvi, "Corporate Management's Inclination to Disclose Financial Information," *Financial Analysts Journal,* July–August, 1972, p. 66.
2. Ibid.
3. Anna Merjos, "Lunch at the Analysts'," *Barron's,* October 8, 1961, p. 5.
4. Victor Niederhoffer and Patrick J. Regan, "Earnings Changes, Analysts' Forecasts and Stock Prices," *Financial Analysts Journal,* May–June, 1972, p. 67.
5. John C. Perham, "The Riddle of the P/E Ratio," *Dun's Review,* September, 1972, p. 40.
6. Martin E. Zweig, "Clouded Crystal Ball," *Barron's,* December 18, 1972, p. 9.
7. Paul E. Dascher, "The Penn Central Revisited: A Predictable Situation," *Financial Analysts Journal,* March–April, 1972, p. 61.
8. Vartanig G. Vartan, "Analyst Recounts Signals in A.T. & T. Turnaround," *New York Times,* December 4, 1972, p. 63.
9. Karen N. Gerard, "Forecasting the Stock Market," in *How Business Economists Forecast,* ed. William F. Butler and Robert A. Kavesh (Prentice-Hall, 1966), p. 494.
10. Beryl W. Sprinkel, *Money and Markets: A Monetarist View* (Richard D. Irwin, 1971), p. 231.

Part II

The News and the General Market

4

Measuring the News

So far we have discussed news in a general way; but in order to determine how, or if, it affects the stock market *as a whole*, it is necessary to devise a way to measure it. The purpose of setting up such a yardstick is obvious: Reliance on mere impressions of whether the news during a given period was good, bad, or indifferent would be suspect at best, as would be any conclusions drawn from them. Unless a system of measurement can be confirmed and put to use by others, it is worth little. Verification is an essential ingredient of the scientific method, and while no one has been able to reduce the study of stock market trends to a science, an investigator at least has the obligation to present his methods for inspection.

The study of records of communication isn't a new one by any means; historians long have pored over musty documents to help them reconstruct the past. During the last century, as the influence and pervasiveness of the mass media have grown, social scientists have tried to go the historians one better by rationalizing the process and giving it a name—content analysis. According to sociologist Bernard Berelson, one of its foremost practitioners, content analysis is "a research technique for the objective, systematic and quantitative description of the manifest content of communication."[1] Defined, "objective" means that standards of analysis must be clearly stated and consistently applied. "Systematic" means that all relevant materials in the body of work selected for study be considered. "Quantitative" means that individual items under study be given a numerical weight that at least roughly corresponds to their importance. This latter step is almost always arbitrary, but it hopefully lends some precision to the results.[2]

Content analysis has been put to work in a wide variety of scholarly projects, but most of them weren't of much direct use to us. In many studies, the focus has been on the actual communications rather than on their effects: how governments whipped up home front patriotic sentiment in wartime, or what magazine biographies tell us about our tastes in heroes over the years, or how educational materials have been presented so school children will retain them.

Most studies of the effects of the mass media, which are our concern, have centered on voting; there have been a large number of attempts to measure how newspaper editorials contributed to the outcome of this or that election. This is more to our point because elections, like broad stock market movements, hinge on the decisions of numerous individuals who are exposed to more or less the same information. The parallel, however, can't be taken too far. We wish to measure how news rather than editorial page exhortations affects behavior, and it easily can be argued that a decision to buy, sell, or keep stocks, or stay out of the market altogether, is a more complex choice than one between two candidates for public office or voting yes or no on a referendum. Given the size of voter turnouts and the comparatively mild tone of American politics, it also can be argued that people take their investment decisions more seriously than their political ones.

Picking the Media

Communications research, however, did help us in planning

our method of attack. The first thing we had to do to relate broad market trends to the news was to find a convenient place to review that news, and for this we picked the *Wall Street Journal*. We will cite other publications, including those put out by brokerage firms, in chapters that show how individual stocks reacted to what was written about them and how stocks reacted to specific news issues. The *Wall Street Journal*, however, seemed the most appropriate place to find the news that was most likely to affect the general market. For one thing, the *Journal* comes every day that the markets are open, and any publication that appears less often would be unlikely to provide the grist for the daily price movements that comprise more general trends. For another, it covers the business scene in more detail than any metropolitan daily or trade paper. Third, it is a national newspaper, reaching investors all over the United States and abroad. Investors in Dayton, Duluth, and Dallas contribute to making the market as well as those in New York, where the most influential of the metropolitan dailies and most of the specialized business presses are based.

The *Journal's* 1972 paid circulation of some 1,250,000 and its estimated readership of about 4.3 million comprised only a fraction of the 32.5 million Americans who owned stocks, but the *Journal* saturates the brokerage and security analyst fields,* and it is to these groups that the majority of investors, including institutions, turn for guidance in their stock trading decisions. A key study of the effects of the mass media on voting identified certain influential individuals in a community as "opinion leaders" who "take material from the formal media and pass it on, with or without distortion or effect, to associates who do not use the formal media so frequently in the particular area of concern."[3] Brokers and analysts certainly are the opinion leaders of the investment community.

National and international news that isn't specifically about business moves the market, too, and while the *Journal* devotes

---

*A 1971 readership study commissioned by the *Journal* showed that 99% of a large sample of financial analysts polled read the paper regularly, and 92% of the group rated it as the "most valuable" publication they read.

much less space to this than do many other newspapers, it provides summaries of major nonbusiness developments in the "World-Wide" column of its daily "What's News" section, which occupies two full columns of its front page. The other "What's News" column, headlined "Business and Finance," supplies one-paragraph summaries of the dozen or so most important business stories that are covered more fully inside the paper. The *Journal* takes its "World-Wide" material from the same Associated Press wires that feed most other U.S. dailies. Thus, its coverage of nonbusiness events mirrors that of the general press. Except for stories of a purely local nature, the *Journal* provides its readers with at least a look at almost all of the morning's significant stories.

Keeping Score

It was to the *Journal's* "What's News" columns that we turned in our effort to evaluate the flow of the daily news. Any attempt to quantify the news must take into account the placement of stories in a publication. In most newspapers, the stories that the editors deem most newsworthy are given the largest headlines on page one, and other stories are placed on that and succeeding pages in descending order of importance. The *Journal's* "What's News" column is entirely on the front page and contains no headlines. This simplified our task of weighting stories by their placement, but it didn't eliminate it. The system we decided upon gave a score of three (3) to the lead, or top, story in both "What's News" columns, a score of two (2) to stories that appear above the fold that divides the paper in half horizontally, and a score of one (1) to stories below the fold. All items in the "What's News" columns were graded except the daily statistical summaries of the previous day's market activity and the "Company Notes" items that appeared occasionally at the end of the "Business and Finance" section.

The *Wall Street Journal* carries three feature stories on its daily front page, and these, too, were taken into account. Features that we deemed potentially market-affecting—usually ones that focused on business or stock market trends—were given a value of three, the same as the lead items in the "What's News" columns.

The system we used to evaluate each day's front page content also was simple: stories that seemed to be good or bullish for the market were given a plus (+); negative or bearish stories got a minus (−); and stories that were neutral or indifferent got a zero (0). A "What's News" lead item or feature that we deemed favorable for stocks received a plus three, a negative lead item or feature a minus three, and so on down.

But as even the most casual investor will appreciate, putting the system into practice was anything but simple. While many kinds of stories were easily categorized—a whopping rise in the gross national product obviously would be good for the market; a big rise in the cost of living would be bad—many others weren't. Corporate price increases, for instance, are good for the companies that get them but bad for ones that must pay. A big increase in defense spending is good for firms that make military hardware, but it might increase the federal budget deficit, which in turn might fuel inflation, and so on.

Before we embarked on our grading process, we solicited the advice of stockbrokers, security analysts, fellow business journalists, economists, and other observers of the business scene. As a test case, we picked six widely chronologically disparate issues of the *Wall Street Journal*, scored them ourselves, and then gave them to fifteen account executives and analysts at three Chicago brokerage offices to grade. We described our grading system to them in general terms and told them to evaluate items solely for their potential impact on stocks generally, all other considerations aside.

Of the 146 gradable items in the six issues, our evaluations matched the majority of the stock market pros on 114, or 78%. Of the 32 items on which we and the pros differed, all but 3 were scored as 0 by our panelists and either plus or minus by us.

In general, the brokers and analysts wrote off as inconsequential internal disputes or changes in government in countries in which the United States had few commercial interests; actions by the government or the courts in such nonbusiness areas as reapportionment, school integration, and narcotics control; government moves short of final decision in business-related subjects (agency studies, congressional committee hearings, and the like); domestic political jockeying; and, perhaps surprisingly, items bearing mainly on the brokerage community, such as those concerning fees, back-office problems, and government regulation of the industry. With the exception of brokerage house failures, which we graded as negative, we followed their lead on those subjects.

In general, our news-grading categories broke down as follows.

Good News

—Upsurges in broad measures of national production, sales, profits, personal income, inventories, capital spending, and employment (unless it was specifically stated that the increases were disappointingly small).

—Increases in production, sales, or contract volume in major individual industries (autos, steel, machine tools, and construction), with the same proviso as above.

—Downward movements of interest rates, broad measures of consumer or wholesale prices, business failures, and unemployment, unless it was clear that an unemployment rate reduction mirrored critical labor shortages.

—Increases in the growth rate of the U.S. money supply.

—Optimistic comments about the near-term state of the U.S. economy by high government officials, economists, or business leaders.

—Reports or forecasts of higher earnings by individual corporations. Here, only the most recent reporting period was considered. For example, if a company reported a second-quarter profit rise but a first-half decline, the item was given a plus.

—Corporate cash dividend increases.

—Corporate plans to increase capital spending or launch major new spending projects.

—Major oil or mineral discoveries by U.S. concerns.

—Reports of federal government budget surpluses or reduced deficits.

—Important steps leading to the approval of major government spending programs.

—The awarding of sizable government contracts to companies.

—Developments that improved prospects for U.S. exports.

—Foreign trade and balance of payments surpluses for the United States.

—Increases in measures of consumer confidence or buying plans.

—Reductions in the price of agricultural commodities and industrial materials, such as metals, fuels, and chemicals.

—Price increases that would be paid mostly by consumers.

—New labor contracts signed on terms deemed favorable to the companies involved.

—Government actions to halt strikes.

—Any resolution or quieting of disputes in foreign countries where the United States had important economic interests.

—Moves toward greater East-West cooperation.

—Agreements to resolve international monetary crises.

—Upturns in stock prices reported in the body of the "Business and Finance" column. (These typically were sizable movements, but they appeared infrequently.)

—Movements of capital away from bank savings accounts and government savings bonds.

—Reports that mutual fund sales topped redemptions in a period.

Bad News

—The opposite of any item listed as good news.

—Any corporate loss in the most recent reporting period.

—Strikes, major layoffs, or plant closings.

—The election of governments considered unfriendly to the United States in countries where the United States had sizable interests.

—Seizures or threatened seizures of U.S. property by foreign governments.

—Moves by foreign governments to increase their share of the revenues of U.S. concerns.

—Large-scale domestic disturbances such as ghetto riots and peace demonstrations that broke into major violence.

Neutral or Unimportant News

—Disputes or changes in government in countries where the United States had few economic interests, government or court actions in nonbusiness areas, other government actions far short of final decision, domestic political jockeying, and most internal stock exchange affairs.

—Routine developments in long-standing foreign conflicts.

—Crimes, accidents, or natural catastrophes that had no clearly stated economic impact.

—Medical news with no clear economic implications.

—Corporate acquisitions, mergers, tender offers, or proxy fights, or their terminations.

—Stock splits or stock dividends that didn't involve increased cash dividends.

—Changes in corporate management.

—Stock swindles, embezzlements, or other financial crimes involving single companies.

—Profit reports by foreign companies.

—The awarding of subcontracts.

—Bill signings and other governmental actions of a ceremonial nature that climaxed developments that had already been determined.

—Highly speculative stories or stories that focused on events in the distant future.

—Purely local matters.

—Stories that combined two or more items that seemed to balance out—company A reports higher profits while company B's earnings dropped.

Some Explanations

The rationale behind our classification of most of the above items should be self-evident, but a few deserve explanation. In considering price increases, for instance, we gave precedence to their short-run effects over any possible long-term implications. Thus, price boosts that would be paid first by individual consumers were graded as pluses, while ones that would affect businesses first (agricultural commodities, fuels, chemicals, metals, and the like) were considered to be negative. Stock market professionals and others we consulted approved of this evaluation.

For the same reason, the approval of major government spending programs got pluses while evidence of mounting federal budget deficits got minuses.

Reports by individual companies of increased sales, earnings, cash dividends, and capital spending plans were accorded pluses, while mergers, acquisitions, stock splits, stock dividends, and management changes were given zeroes because we believed that the former group of actions were more reflective of broad economic trends than the latter group, and thus were more likely to affect the general market.

It is frequently said that Wall Street hates uncertainty, and we used this as a guide in grading the news surrounding the international monetary crises that dotted our periods of concern. Accordingly, events signaling the onset of monetary realignments (increased speculation in gold and currency fluctuations on foreign markets) were graded as minuses while the agreements that temporarily resolved the flare-ups were regarded as good news, even if they had some unpleasant implications for the U.S. economy.

The War in Vietnam: A Special Case

As we will explain in more detail later, news of the American war effort in Vietnam played an important role in stock price movements during the periods on which we concentrated. Stock market observers agreed that in the early phases of the war, news of increased U.S. commitments to the South Vietnamese were considered bullish and were greeted by stock market rallies centering on defense issues. By about the middle of 1966, however, it had become apparent that the war was overheating the U.S. economy and raising the specters of accelerated inflation, balance-of-payments deficits, and increased government controls on business, 'all of which eventually came to pass. Accompanying this was a degree of domestic turmoil unmatched in recent American history.

Accordingly, beginning with the stock market downturn of

1966, we began giving plus ratings to stories of apparent movements toward peace and U.S. troop withdrawals, and minuses to
escalations of the conflict by either side. Routine battlefield developments were given zeroes throughout.

Measuring the Market

Our barometer of stock price movements was the Dow Jones
Industrial Average. We selected it with full knowledge that it is an
imperfect tool with which to gauge broad stock-price trends. It is
composed of only 30 blue-chip stocks listed on the New York Stock
Exchange and, as such, is far less inclusive than other widely used
indexes. Also, the DJIA has become increasingly volatile as the
divisor used to compute it has shrunk with every stock split or
stock dividend issued by constituent companies. Indeed, it was a
good deal more volatile than our News Index, and this presented
us with problems of comparability.

On the other hand, studies have shown that no serious distortion of stock market trends results from the use of the DJIA. Just
as importantly, it is by far the most popular measurement of
market activity. In fact, when analysts and newsmen comment on
the direction of the market, they usually mean the DJIA. We felt
that using any other average would force us into frequent and burdensome explanations.

Limitations and Problems

One limitation of our system of scoring the news was that the
morning's *Wall Street Journal* often didn't contain all the news
that could affect the market that day. Late editions of the *Journal*
go to press at about 10 P.M., so any events that took place after that
did not make the paper. Typically, reports of such events were
transmitted by the business news wire services during the trading
day and appeared in the next day's *Journal*.

Because of this, we felt that any attempt to gauge the effect of
the published morning news on daily stock-price movements
would fall seriously short, so we based our stock-price news calculations on weekly measurements of both. This, too, had its draw-

backs—market movements on Fridays may have stemmed from news that wasn't reported until after the day's *Journal* was in print —but we believed that a weekly period at least minimized the impact of such occurrences.

One drawback of our scoring system was that it might not have given sufficient weight to single, very important developments that affected the market for days or weeks. Henry Kissinger's statement in late October, 1972, that peace in Vietnam was at hand, was one example, touching off a rally that lasted into early 1973. It was our observation, however, that very important developments typically are commented upon, explained, and revised for many days after they take place, and thus appear in the news again and again for further evaluation. Moreover, as we said before, any effort to quantify anything as complex as news is necessarily arbitrary, and we could conceive of no system that could finely evaluate every grade of event.

The problem of ambiguity was further brought home to us when we tried to find out if others saw the news the same way we did. We tested this by turning over our detailed list of grading criteria to two fellow business reporters and a retired business executive and asked them to score the daily *Wall Street Journal* "What's News" columns of March and April, 1973, as they appeared. We also graded the same papers.

Of a total of 1,209 gradable items in 42 issues, our evaluations were the same as theirs, 89.8% of the time. In just 1.1% of the cases, we scored an item as plus and one of our volunteers gave it a minus, or vice versa. While we considered these percentages to be satisfactory, the differences did point out the difficulties involved in applying our criteria evenly.

Finally, it has been suggested that perhaps the movements of the stock market affect the news, instead of the other way around. According to this view, editors may place stories in a way that accentuates good news when the market is rising and bad news when it is falling. Experience tells us that this isn't true in any significant way. Even if it were, it wouldn't reverse our equation. If the Wall Street pros and others are correct in telling us that what people *think* is true is what really matters, newspaper editors aren't the only ones whose perceptions are subject to such distortion.

Applying the News Index

We relied mainly on the quantitative approach in matching general stock market trends to the flow of the news in Chapters 5, 6, and 7. Chapter 5 sketches the overall pattern of the market from late 1965 to early 1972 and focuses closely on the four major upturns that took place in that period. Chapter 6 zeroes in on the four most important downturns taken by stocks. Chapter 7 looks at the pattern of news and stocks during 1972.

We chose to concentrate on a recent time period because we believed it would be most relevant to contemporary market observers. Chapters 5 and 6 are concerned with turnaround periods because of their importance to investors and because they have long been the most difficult for analysts of all persuasions to predict. We wanted to see if they could have been foretold by systematic attention to the news.

For both the upturns and the downturns, we began our news analysis six weeks before the market turned and continued it for six weeks afterward. That seemed to us to be sufficient time to judge how, or if, the direction of stock prices followed news trends. Chapter 7 focuses on an entire year to determine how the news and the market interacted during a more normal period of time.

We submitted our weekly news market data for all three chapters to computer analysis, and while it turned out that market movements usually were related to News Index changes, the relationships were too weak to have any predictive value. In broader terms, however, we think our results were more substantial, as we will spell out in detail.

Notes

1. Bernard Berelson, "Content Analysis," in *Handbook of Social Psychology*, vol. 1, ed. Gardner Lindzey (Addison-Wesley, 1954), p. 489.
2. Claire Sellitz et. al., *Research Methods in Social Relations* (Henry Holt, 1959), p. 336.
3. Paul Lazarsfeld, Bernard Berelson, and Helen Gaudet, *The People's Choice: How the Voter Makes Up His Mind in a Presidential Campaign* (Duell, Sloan and Pierce, 1944), p. 49.

5

Four Upturns

THE stock market took eight major turns in the six-year period from late December 1965 to early January 1972, but the net effect of the market's meanderings in all of that time was virtually nil. On December 27, 1965, the Dow Jones Industrial Average closed at 960, and on January 7, 1972, it closed at 910. In between, the average fell and rose in roughly a 350-point range.

Market plateaus are to be expected from time to time. They occurred in 1947–49, 1951–53 and 1955–57, for instance. Like the 1965–72 period, these were times of considerable social and economic change. The big difference was that as the DJIA climbed higher, the plateaus themselves became more irregular—the result of the Dow becoming a more volatile index, as mentioned before, and the dominance of institutional trading. The upshot was the 350-point range of the 1965–72 plateau, whereas in 1951–53 the Dow ranged only from 235 to 295.

One explanation for the market's lackluster performance in the 1965–72 period was that corporate profits lost their upward

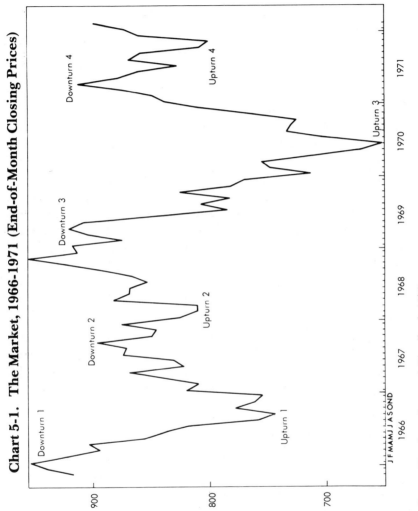

Chart 5-1. The Market, 1966-1971 (End-of-Month Closing Prices)

Source: Dow Jones Investor's Handbook, 1973.

thrust of the early 1960s. The government's chart of corporate profits and the chart of the Dow look almost the same during this six-year span. Not until 1972 did corporate profits rise higher than the 1966 peak of $50 billion, and it was in 1972 that the Dow broke through the 1,000 level.

Some analysts think corporate profits and the stock market both were victims of the winds of social change that at times blew at hurricane strength during this period. The war in Vietnam was, of course, a central event; not only did it help accelerate inflation but it turned dissidents, especially the young, against the established order. Antagonism was directed toward big corporations as well as the government and the military. Concurrent forces such as consumerism and environmentalism added to the criticism heaped on business. Big companies became whipping boys for many social and political ills.

Other analysts point out that during this period the stock market ceased being the only investment game in town for some people. Conservative investors began turning to high-yield corporate bonds. Prior to 1965, yields for long-term bonds didn't come close to matching the gains available in stocks. By the early 1970s, bond rates climbed 7.5% and higher and, consequently, gained in appeal. More daring types discovered that trading commodity futures, international currencies, and other speculations could be at least as profitable (sometimes more so) and often more adventuresome than trading stocks. Finally, changes in capital gains tax laws diminished some of the allure the stock market previously held for many investors.

How the News Flowed

We expected the interplay of these factors to show up in sometimes dramatic shifts in the flow of the news from positive to negative and back again. Such was the case, with predictable results for the market.

Table 5-A shows the extent to which the News Index leaned toward the positive or negative in the six weeks before and after the four major upturns of the 1965–72 period. For the most part, the news in the six-week periods before each upturn was negative. The only exception was the period leading to the 1971–72 rally, when there was one more positive news day than negative news day; the index split evenly between positive and negative weeks, however. In the 24 weeks that preceded the four upturns, the news was negative 62% of the days, positive 29%, and neutral 9%. Measured by weeks, the news was positive 25% of the time and negative 75%.

Table 5-A. News Flow before and after Major Upturns

| | News Index | | | | | |
| | Number of Days | | | Number of Weeks | | |
	+	−	0	+	−	0
Upturn 1 (1966)						
6 weeks before upturn	5	18	6	1	5	0
6 weeks after upturn	15	9	4	4	2	0
Upturn 2 (1968)						
6 weeks before upturn	9	16	4	2	4	0
6 weeks after upturn	21	6	3	6	0	0
Upturn 3 (1970)						
6 weeks before upturn	5	25	0	0	6	0
7 weeks after upturn	17	15	3	4	3	0
Upturn 4 (1971–72)						
6 weeks before upturn	15	14	0	3	3	0
6 weeks after upturn	24	6	0	6	0	0
Totals						
Before upturns	34	73	10	6	18	0
After upturns	77	36	10	20	5	0

The news was predominantly positive in the first weeks of the fledgling bull markets. In the 1970 upturn the margin of positive over negative days was much narrower than in the others, and the market did not gain as fast. In the first 25 weeks of the four newly rising markets* the News Index was positive 63% of the days, negative 29%, and neutral 8%—virtually the exact opposite of the preupturn period. In terms of weeks, the news was positive 80% of the time.

The conclusion seems inescapable: When the flow of the news abruptly reverses itself from very negative to very positive, the market is bound to stop falling and start rising. Of course, when the market goes up, some individual stocks may not; but in a rising market, where gainers outnumber losers—sometimes three or four to one—investors have a much better chance of picking stocks that will appreciate in value. There didn't seem to be a set pattern to whether the shift in the news flow preceded the upturn —as it did in two of the cases—or if it coincided with or lagged slightly behind the change in market direction. What was clear was that the market quickly responded to the sudden, steady gush of good news that seems to be a bull's best friend.

The Upturn of 1966

The year 1966 was in many ways a difficult one, and for nine months the market reflected the nagging uncertainties about the Vietnam war, inflation, and continued economic growth. These matters were mulled over almost daily in brokerage newsletters, investment advisories, and the business press by late August, which is when we began grading the news for this first market upturn. More than a month of steadily negative news fed these bearish broodings, and eventually the market fell.

Then, in early October, the news suddenly turned positive. The following week the market turned upward, beginning what was to be a 200-point, 27% rise. The news continued to be positive for a month, then dipped negative for a week, then positive, and then negative again; the market zigzagged in response. Chart 5-2 graphically shows the movements of the News Index and the Dow, indicating that the news turned positive a bit before the market turned bullish.

---

*We extended the postupturn period by an extra week in 1970 to validate the trends of the News Index and the market.

Chart 5-2.　Upturn of 1966

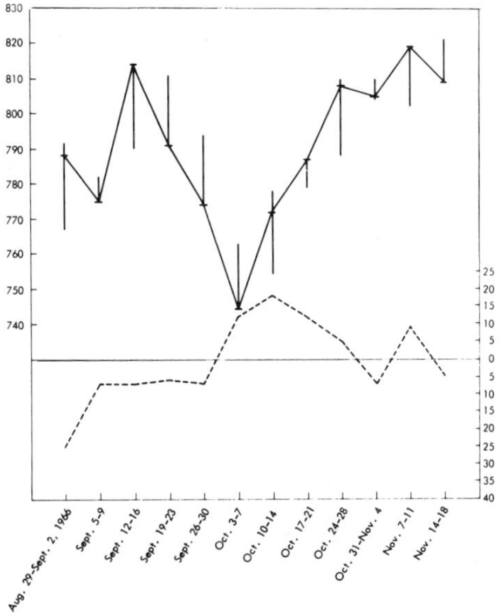

The recurring bad news theme in our first five weeks was inflation and its companion, tight money. Not only were interest rates climbing, but some companies couldn't borrow money at any price. In its August 31 issue, the *Journal* reported that Montgomery Ward said high interest rates were cutting into its earnings; on September 7, a survey of corporations revealed that tight money was prompting businessmen to cut back their expansion plans for 1967. On September 1, Chrysler grumped that tight money probably would hold down 1967 auto sales, and on September 14 and 23 it was reported that, indeed, sales of new cars were declining. Experts were quoted as citing tight money as one reason why they expected housing starts to continue falling in the foreseeable future, and banks said they also were being bruised in the money crunch.

Of course, the news wasn't all bad. One item of good news was credited with sparking the 39-point rally in the third week that ran counter to the dominating flow of bad news. On Friday, September 9, President Johnson's Administration announced several efforts to curb inflation, including repealing the 7% investment tax credit that had spurred capital spending by business. That struck a responsive chord in at least some quarters, and on the following Monday, September 12, the market spurted 15 points, followed by gains of 5 points on Tuesday, 11 points on Wednesday, and 8 points on Thursday.

But even as the market was climbing, some analysts recognized that this strand of good news was too thin to support a full-fledged turnaround: "Until the Johnson proposals are honed out in detail, passed by Congress and produce some result in this exercise in push-button economics, I would view this as just a rally—not a sustained recovery move," one analyst said in the *Journal's* "Abreast of the Market" column of September 13.

Sure enough, the market couldn't keep rising in the face of continued bad news. In the next three weeks it plunged 70 points to 744 on October 7, the lowest level since 1963.

The week the market bottomed out began with bad news, but by the end of the week the news had become favorable. On Friday, October 7, there were several good-news items, including a report that sales of 1967-model cars were off to a surprisingly good start despite the fretting about expected declines. Other items: a government economist predicted a slowdown in inflation in 1967, and the major retail chains set a sales record in September.

The market responded the following Monday with a rise of more than 10 points. The news was again good on Tuesday, and the market gained 4 points. On Wednesday, October 12, the market spurted nearly 20 points. The action began about 1:30 P.M. with statements by top Johnson administration officials that the Vietnam war wouldn't require direct wage-price controls, followed by the secretary of state expressing hope of reaching some key diplomatic agreements with the Soviet Union.

"The White House was really turning on the good news," commented an analyst in "Abreast of the Market" the next morning.

And so the market turned, sustained by good news. The news

turned negative the first week in November, and the market dipped in sympathy; key items were a slowdown in new car sales, an increase in nickel prices, and an observation by retailers that consumers were becoming somewhat cautious. But the following week good news returned, and the market rebounded. In the third week of November, the news turned sour again, and once more the market eased. This time the items were more ominous: signs of a business slowdown had heightened and chances for a favorable U.S. trade balance, the government said, were dimming because of the Vietnam war. Nevertheless, the market advanced for the next ten months, albeit with hesitation.

The Upturn of 1968

Sudden, momentous events hardly ever trigger major turns in the market. President Kennedy's assassination in 1963, for instance, caused just a momentary lapse in the bull market of 1962–66, and the impact of the Arab-Israeli Six-Day War, in June 1967, was equally transitory, in the short run. Sometimes big news gets credit for precipitating a basic shift in market direction because the news and the shift occur at the same time, but a closer look usually reveals that a change in the *flow* of the news is responsible.

Such is the case with our second upturn (see Chart 5-3). The market had been falling since late September 1967, and by mid-February 1968, when we began the news grading, it was drifting lower aimlessly. Then, beginning in April, it shot up like a rocket. The big news was President Johnson's Vietnam peace initiative, which led to the Paris talks, and his accompanying announcement that he wouldn't run for a second full term. Important as it was, that single event wasn't enough to propel the market into a new long-term trend, although it probably accelerated the pace of the upturn at its beginning.

From mid-February through mid-March the news was overwhelmingly negative. Inflation was heating up and the head of the Federal Reserve System warned of the need for wage-price con-

Chart 5-3. Upturn of 1968

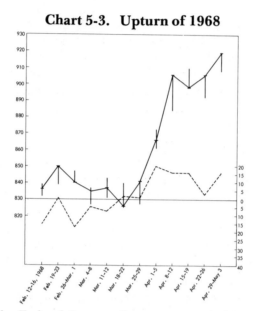

trols; then the Federal Reserve System proceeded to tighten credit. In Vietnam, General Westmoreland was asking a war-weary nation for more and more troops, and LBJ was sending them.

Largely because of the war, the United States was spending more abroad than it was taking in. This caused a severe drain on U.S. gold reserves and prompted speculators in Europe and elsewhere to bid up the price of gold on the hunch that the United States couldn't long afford to keep its official price pegged at $35 an ounce. By Thursday, March 14, the gold situation had reached critical proportions and the market fell 11 points.

Over the weekend, the international monetary chiefs devised a two-tier gold-pricing system whereby the $35 price would remain for governmental transactions but the general market price, governed by supply and demand, would be allowed to float freely. The gold crisis abated and the News Index, reflecting this development, turned positive. But the market continued downward and hit its trough of 825 on March 21. The following week the market rebounded 14 points on the second consecutive week of good news.

The fireworks began with President Johnson's March 31 announcements. The market shot up nearly 21 points on Monday and gained an additional 11 points through Thursday. A seven-point correction came on Friday—the day after Martin Luther King, Jr., was killed and riots erupted in several cities—but on the following Monday the market gained almost 19 points.

Some analysts thought these jumps were too much too soon and that they wouldn't be sustained. "The market now is vulnerable to bad news, which is just the reverse of the situation a week ago when it was vulnerable to good news," remarked one in the "Abreast of the Market" column on April 4.

But there was a lot more good news. Hanoi responded favorably to President Johnson's peace initiative and the Paris peace talks were set up. The market pulsated with each announcement or rumor that made peace seem closer. We would argue, though, that a market rally based solely on peace news of such a tentative nature would have fizzled sooner or later.

That it didn't, we think, is attributable to the flow of good economic news that had begun two weeks before the blockbuster headlines and continued thereafter. Here are some of the key economic items in the weeks beginning April 1: machine tool orders increased; construction spending rose; major retailers' sales went up; higher earnings were reported by several big companies; record business spending was predicted; and personal disposable income continued to advance. It would be difficult to imagine the market going anywhere but up on news such as this, especially when it was also buttressed by favorable international developments.

Even when banks raised the prime rate during the week of April 22–26, reminding everybody that inflation was still a problem, there was enough good news to keep the index positive. Later on, of course, inflation, tight money, and international monetary problems returned to haunt the market.

The Upturn of 1970

Sometimes the market turns in times of turbulence, when the

underlying news flow is obscured. Such was the case with this third upturn, which ended the 1969–70 bear market. These three events made the biggest headlines during the April–July news-grading period: President Nixon sent U.S. troops to invade Cambodia; four students were killed at Kent State University, crystalizing the emotional rifts and social turmoil generated by the Vietnam conflict; and the Penn Central Railroad, the nation's largest, plunged into bankruptcy. These stories gave the news an outwardly negative cast even when such an interpretation was no longer justified. As Chart 5-4 shows, as the News Index climbed from its negative depths and broke into the positive range, the market responded by first halting its decline and then rebounding. This was an instance in which close attention to the basic flow of the news could have paid off in an early spotting of a new bull market.

The news was exceedingly gloomy for more than a month that spring while the market steadily sank. Corporate earnings were falling, two major labor strikes were in progress, and such economic indicators as factory orders and construction spending were dropping. Perversely, the only things going up were interest rates, the prices of steel and many other items, unemployment, labor costs, and the federal budget deficit.

"There just doesn't seem to be an end to this lousy market," bemoaned one broker in the *Journal*'s "Abreast of the Market" column on April 24. Added another: "You keep hearing that the bad news is already discounted, but many stocks take a beating anyway."

It is little wonder, then, that the Cambodian invasion, which raised the specter of a wider war in Southeast Asia, hit the market hard. The *Journal*'s "Abreast of the Market" column gave this account of the market's performance on Monday, May 4, three days after the invasion was announced:

> Pushed by international tensions, the stock market tobogganed yesterday as the Dow Jones Industrial average sustained its sharpest drop since the day President Kennedy was shot in 1963. . . . Plunging 19.07 points, the industrial average closed at 714.56. . . . The market

Chart 5-4.   Upturn of 1970

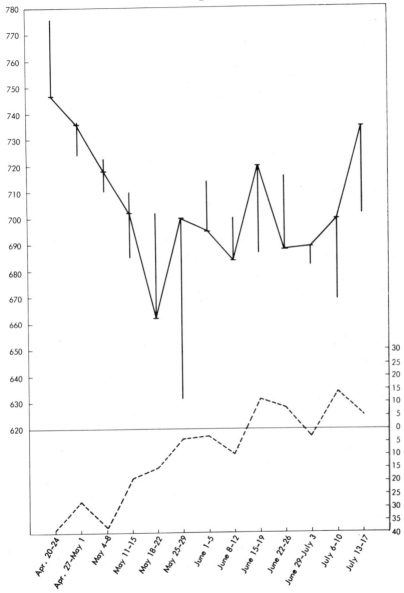

headed down right from the opening . . . following news that Russian Premier Kosygin would hold a press conference later in the morning to comment on the U.S.'s military campaign into Cambodia. The average showed a loss of 14.91 points at 11:30 A.M. But, as one broker commented, "Kosygin's remarks proved to be more diplomatic and less threatening than had been expected." Prices then began to recover and by 12:30 P.M. the industrial average had trimmed its loss to 7.92 points. But the statement shortly after noon by Communist China terming the U.S. intervention in Cambodia a "provocation" to the Chinese people then began to depress the market. Prices started diving again. Brokers said discouragement generated by the failure of the noon rally to get very far increased the downward pressure. Still another burden was the news that four persons were killed and at least 12 wounded by gunfire . . . at Kent State University.

But after this initial shock the market didn't react much further to the Cambodian venture, which was shortly terminated. The market was hammered instead by a fresh onslaught of bad economic news, including a sharp drop in housing starts and machine tool orders. The market plunged to its May 26 low of 631 on such news, helped by distress selling by investors whose margin-account equity had been eroded by the falling market and who needed to sell shares at any price to pay off margin calls.

Interestingly, though, good-news items began popping up just as the bear market hit bottom. There wasn't enough good news to tip the index positive, but the items were significant: factory orders for durable goods rose in April (reported in the May 22 issue); auto sales improved unexpectedly in mid-May (May 25); mortgage interest rates fell in April for the first time in 17 months (May 26). And on May 29, this flood of good news: President Nixon predicted an economic upturn in the second half of 1970; money market rates declined; auto makers showed their optimism by building inventories; and construction contracts rose a surprising 15% in April.

The market picked up and responded to those positive notes, though the News Index itself remained negative. But in the week of June 15–19, the news turned positive for the first time, and the market jumped. The key item concerned a slowdown in the rate of inflation. The news continued to be positive the following week, but the market fell in response to the collapse of the Penn Central Railroad into bankruptcy—a case in which an important event wasn't realistically measured by the News Index. Rumors floated wildly around Wall Street that other corporations could be hit with financial problems, too, though few of these materialized.

During the next week the News Index turned negative, largely the result of one day's bad news. Then good news returned and the market began to climb. We stretched the grading period through a thirteenth week to see what would happen. Sure enough, the news remained positive—auto sales were stronger than expected, second-quarter profits were up at many companies, housing starts rose—and the market shot up. It climbed 51% in eleven months to a high of 950 before falling again.

Strictly speaking, the News Index didn't turn positive before the market actually touched bottom, but the news had improved markedly by that period. More to the point, it wasn't until the News Index did turn positive that the market scored any significant advances and that the upturn really got under way.

The Upturn of 1971–72

In some cases it isn't so much bad news that sends the market down as it is uncertainty; when those uncertainties are resolved, the market turns up.

Chart 5-5 shows uncertainty as portrayed by the News Index— a weekly wavering between positive and negative for the first six weeks of the grading period. Much of the economic news was good. Many companies were reporting third-quarter profit increases; the prime interest rate dropped from 6% to 5¾% and then to 5½%; auto sales were at record levels; and retailers said they were expecting strong Christmas sales gains.

But the bad news was unsettling. Steel orders were lagging and the big steelmakers posted third-quarter deficits or sharply

Chart 5-5. Upturn of 1971-72

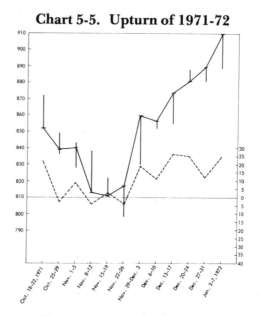

lower earnings; a European recession threatened to hamper the U.S. economy's slow recovery from its own 1970 recession; and several key economic indicators kept easing downward.

In addition, there were two especially nagging items. First, Phase 2 economic control rules were being announced during this period and it took people several weeks to figure out what they were all about. Second, one of the more serious international monetary crises was brewing. It had become evident that to be workable any currency realignment would require formal devaluation of the U.S. dollar. People wondered if President Nixon would agree to such a move, and whether the countries with the upper hand would try somehow to extract an extra pound of flesh.

These crosswinds of good news and bad news also had an impact because of the technical condition of the market. The small investors had practically deserted the market and left the big institutional investors with no one to absorb the shares they wanted to sell; when they unloaded even tiny blocks, the Dow would drop sharply. During this period, mutual fund redemptions were exceeding purchases, so the funds had to sell shares to pay off the customers who were bailing out.

The market hit its low of 798 on Tuesday, November 23. It gained slightly on Wednesday; but on Friday, the day after Thanksgiving, it jumped nearly 18 points; the next week it climbed 43 points. The news began a distinctly positive trend on Wednesday, but this wasn't reflected in the News Index until Friday. Thereafter, the news retained its strongly positive tone into 1972.

The general economic news didn't change much after Thanksgiving, it was about as good as it had been before. The difference was that the uncertainties began to be resolved in the right direction. The White House began spreading the word that it was working toward monetary accord, which it predicted would come before the end of the year. Devaluing the dollar wasn't the hangup that some had expected. As December rolled around, it appeared that the Price Commission and Wage Board probably would have some short-run success in restraining inflation without puncturing the business recovery. And Europe's recession didn't seem to be having much effect in the United States after all.

Another change in the news came in the context of outlook stories. In the first six weeks, before the upturn, the forward-lookers had their doubts. Business leaders at a fall conference said they were less optimistic than they had been about future economic gains, steelmakers began voicing doubts that an order surge predicted for January would materialize, and auto makers said they didn't think the car-buying boom would last long.

But after Thanksgiving, outlook stories were much more bullish: a Federal agency predicted an 8.5% gain in capital spending in the first half of 1972; a steel-buying pickup for the first quarter of 1972 was reforecast; a survey of economists turned up general predictions of strong business gains in 1972; and various experts said they expected interest rates to go down.

So, as soon as the clouds were cleared away—as reflected in a decisive shift of the News Index to steadily positive—the market pulled out of its decline.

6

Four Downturns

THE stock market suffered four extended setbacks during the 1966–1971 period.

In the eight months between February 9 and October 7, 1966, the DJIA declined 26% from 995 (its all-time closing high up to that time) to 744.

In the six months between September 25, 1967, and March 21, 1968, the DJIA dropped 13% from 943 to 825.

In the 12½ months between May 14, 1969, and May 26, 1970, the index dived 35% from 969 to 631.* This was the longest and most severe decline of the post-World War II years.

In the seven months between April 28 and November 23, 1971, the average dropped 18% from 951 to 798.

When we set out to analyze the flow of the news for the six-

---

*The market reached its true peak for that period in November 1968, when it touched the 980s. It declined to around 900 in early December, then moved upward again until May 1969.

week periods leading up to the market peaks, we expected to find that the news had already turned negative, although perhaps not overwhelmingly so. We reasoned that the seeds of any major downturn would be evident even before the downturn itself began. The vast majority of the investing public, including institutions as well as individuals, buys stocks in the expectation that they will rise in price. We are (or were) a nation of optimists, and our national history has lent credence to the belief that conditions will improve over the long haul. We thus expected investor optimism to persist until evidence to the contrary—as reflected in the news—made that position untenable.

We expected that the news in the first six weeks of our extended bear markets would be strongly negative. Even in periods of advance, the stock market frequently experiences setbacks of several weeks in duration. We reasoned that the difference between a minor and major reversal would be a sustained, severe dose of bad news. The results of the application of our News Index to the four downturns are summarized in Table 6–A.

As is evident, the flow of the news in the weeks preceding the downturns varied widely. In two of them (1966 and 1971), the market peaked on mostly good news; in the other two (1967–68 and 1969–70) the news was mostly bad as stocks staged what was to be their final rally. For the 24 weeks prior to the four major downward moves, the News Index was positive for 42% of the weeks, negative for 50%, and zero for 8%. On a daily basis, the News Index was positive 46% of the time, negative 45%, and neutral 9%. Again, the index did not prove to be a strong predictive device.

But the flow of the news in the first six weeks of the four major declines was solidly and overwhelmingly negative, as we had expected. In the 24 weeks after the stock market had reached its peaks, the news was bad in 23 weeks and good in only one; daily, the News Index was negative 73% of the time, positive 20%, and neutral 7%.

Such stretches of almost unrelievedly bad news are decidedly unusual. In the next chapter, which spells out the relationship of

Table 6-A.   News Flow before and after Major Downturns

| | News Index | | | | | |
| | Number of Days | | | Number of Weeks | | |
	+	−	0	+	−	0
Downturn 1 (1966)						
6 weeks before downturn	17	10	3	3	2	1
6 weeks after downturn	6	19	4	1	5	0
Downturn 2 (1967–68)						
6 weeks before downturn	11	14	4	1	4	1
6 weeks after downturn	5	22	3	0	6	0
Downturn 3 (1969–70)						
6 weeks before downturn	11	18	1	1	5	0
6 weeks after downturn	6	22	1	0	6	0
Downturn 4 (1971)						
6 weeks before downturn	16	11	3	5	1	0
6 weeks after downturn	6	22	1	0	6	0
Totals						
Before downturns	55	53	11	10	12	2
After downturns	23	85	9	1	23	0

the News Index to the stock market movements of 1972, which wasn't marked by a major downturn, we encountered only one period in which the news was negative for as long as three consecutive weeks. Thus, we can conclude that just as stock prices cannot continue to decline in the face of consistently good news, they also cannot continue to advance against news that is consistently bad. An investor who trimmed his portfolio six weeks into all four of the downturns would have avoided the brunt of his potential losses.

Such knowledge can have important investment implications, of course. The most widely adopted posture during bear markets is defensive; investors typically sell stocks and put their money into corporate or government bonds or bank certificates of deposit. At the same time, bear markets also present profit opportunities to the stouthearted. One may sell short or purchase options to sell, called "puts," both of which anticipate the sort of substantial declines in the price of individual stocks that accompany all bear markets. It is not our purpose to explain these maneuvers in detail —such information is readily available elsewhere. Suffice it to say that despite Bernard Baruch's widely quoted statement that "bears don't live on Park Avenue" and the unpatriotic connotations that have been attached to short selling tactics, the smiling bear is not an endangered species.

The Downturn of 1966

In the last week of December 1965, the stock market was in the final phase of an advance that had begun in the middle of 1962, fully three and a half years before. The Dow Jones Industrial Average went into the week of December 27 at 966, a rise of 431 points from its 1962 low of 535. As of this writing in mid-1973, it was the last of the truly sustained bull markets.

As Chart 6-1 shows, the market had only one strong rally left as 1966 dawned. The week of January 3–7 it rose 17 points to close at 986. For the next four weeks it remained virtually stationary. Between February 7 and 9 it moved up 9 points to its closing-price peak of 995, but it declined swiftly thereafter.

The news in the six weeks prior to the decline was mostly good, at least on the surface. On December 27, the nation's major steel producers announced that they would boost operations in 1966 and hire more workers. In a front-page story titled "Happy New Year," the *Wall Street Journal* of December 29 said that economists who had been questioned predicted the economy would continue to expand strongly in 1966, although perhaps not at quite as strong a clip as it had in 1965.

The following day, the newspaper said in another front-page story that President Johnson was planning to go to Congress with requests to spend a lot more money for men and arms to pursue

Chart 6-1. Downturn of 1966

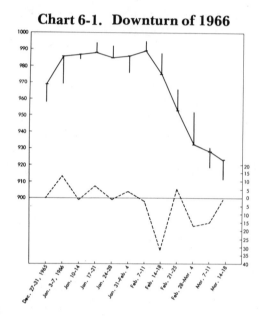

the war in Vietnam. Defense stocks bounded upward on the news.

In the first three weeks of 1966, government economic statistics for the previous year began to flow in, and the news again was good. The gross national product in 1965 totaled $675 billion, a 7.5% rise from 1964. Construction outlays during the year had set a record. Auto makers expected another banner year, a *Wall Street Journal* survey of dealers indicated. Factory orders hit a record in November. Industrial production hit a record in December. Corporate profits were strong, although they were advancing more slowly than in the previous few years.

Even in the midst of all this, however, a reader could find ominous notes. There were warnings that the economy was overheating in the face of strong domestic demand coupled with the escalating war effort. Consumer prices, which had risen at an annual rate of just 1.2% in the preceding few years, were climbing faster. The Consumer Price Index rose in November, and the December figure also was expected to be up, the *Wall Street Journal* reported on December 31.

Also in the last week of December, it was announced that construction awards dropped in November, the first monthly decline since February. The *Journal* of December 30 quoted a speech in which Gardner Ackley, chairman of the President's Council of Economic Advisers, warned that the economy was operating close to capacity in terms of both plant and employment. "At some point the economy will really be operating at the ceiling set by labor-force growth and the advance of productivity," Mr. Ackley said. "The growth of real output cannot forever be as fast as we have had during the past several years and as we project for the coming year."

Industrial price increases also crowded into the spotlight. At the first of the year, Bethlehem Steel raised prices on its structural products by $5 a ton, an increase so large that it incurred the displeasure of the president. A few days later, U.S. Steel raised its prices of structurals by just $2.75 a ton, forcing Bethlehem to cut back to that level. Initially, this was seen as good news; the White House applauded and the stock market moved up 12 points on January 5, with steels leading the way. Within a week, however, it became apparent that the price hike would fall heavily on the building industry, hastening a decline in construction activity that already was in progress.

By late January, the good news, which had consisted mostly of reports of what had happened in 1965, was just about exhausted. On January 24, LBJ presented a whopping deficit budget to Congress, and aides hinted that additional taxes might be necessary. On January 27 it was revealed that living costs in December had taken their sharpest monthly increase in 15 years. Interest rates on U.S. Treasury notes hit 5% for the first time in many years, indicating tough times ahead in the money markets.

In February, more bad news. In a February 7 story, the *Journal* reported that members of the National Association of Purchasing Agents, who had seen an accelerated number of price increases cross their desks, said that "inflation looms as a more serious threat than it has been in many years." January unemployment dipped to 4%, its lowest level in nine years;

usually this would be good news but this time it accentuated the realization that the labor market had become dangerously tight.

Once the February 9 peak had been reached, the market dropped sharply. It was off 14 points the week of February 14, 22 points the next week, and 21 points the third. The news ran counter to the trend only during the week of February 21, when several large corporations reported strong 1965 results.

However, the next week the news was negative again. By March, price increases had spread to chemicals and copper, and the steel companies raised their prices again. Unemployment in February was down to 3.7%, and labor shortages loomed ever larger. On March 10, major banks in New York, Chicago, and Pittsburgh raised their prime interest rate to 5¼%, the highest level since the 1930s. No more need be said.

The Downturn of 1967–68

The stock market reversal that began in late September 1967 was the mildest (13%) and the briefest of the four that occurred between 1966 and the end of 1971. It also was the one with perhaps the least economic justification.

Although the downturn of 1966 wasn't accompanied by any marked contraction of the economy as a whole, the composite index of leading indicators was in slight decline during much of the year, and several of its constituents—notably private housing starts, net business formations and the rate of growth of consumer installment debt—dropped by substantial amounts. In contrast, almost all major measures of economic activity rose in the late 1967, early 1968 period, albeit irregularly.

The general news scene in the months encompassing that slide, however, was one of deep and disquieting uncertainty. U.S. troop strength in Vietnam had grown to 525,000, American planes were bombing close to the Chinese border, and domestic opposition to the war was mounting, both in Congress and on the streets and campuses. President Johnson had recommended a tax surcharge to pay for the growing costs of the war, only stirring more debate. Consumer prices were continuing their upward

Chart 6-2. Downturn of 1967-68

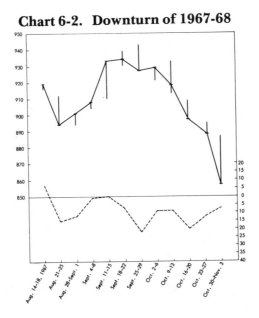

march, and labor unions responded by pressing for larger wage increases. On the other side of the world, Israel and its Arab enemies were glaring at one another over the cease-fire lines created by Israel's victory in the Six-Day War of three months before. The effect of all this could only be depressing to investors.

There was, of course, some good news as stocks moved toward their September 25 peak of 943. In mid-August, the government reported that corporate profits gained in the second quarter. Auto companies were predicting that their sales in 1968 would top those of 1967. Record crops of corn, soybeans, and wheat were predicted by the Agriculture Department as harvest time approached. There was even an encouraging development on the international scene —on August 24, the United States and the Soviet Union reached agreement in Geneva on a draft treaty to prevent the spread of nuclear arms.

Mostly, though, the news was bad in the six weeks before the peak. As in the early days of the 1966 downturn, key industrial prices were moving up. The *Wall Street Journal* of August 24 devoted a front-page story to recently instituted boosts in the price of chemicals, steel, aluminum, rubber tires, and construction materials. The *Journal* said the outlook for a reversal of the upward trend was dim in light of the proposed tax surcharge, which would accentuate pressure on profits.

Interest rates, that bugaboo of the market, also were on the rise; in late August, mortgage rates climbed to 6% after a few months of easing. On September 6, the United Auto Workers struck Ford, casting a note of uncertainty over the auto companies' previous optimism.

The market made its last upward thrust the week of September 11–15, gaining 26 points. It was a move that experts were hard pressed to explain. The move was "inflation motivated," ventured one analyst on September 14 in "Abreast of the Market"— investors were rushing to get out of cash and into securities in the face of spiraling prices, he said.

The news turned strongly negative the week before the market went into its dive. In the week of September 18, prices of nickel and chemicals rose, as did consumer prices. On the 20th, the *Journal* carried the news that factory orders dropped in August for the second straight month. The same day's newspapers quoted U Thant, secretary-general of the United Nations, as saying that a broader war might develop in the Middle East if his organization didn't move swiftly to calm Israeli-Arab tensions.

It was more of the same the next week. The *Journal* focused new attention on rising prices in a front-page article titled "Unseen Inflation," which chronicled the boosts in individual prices that were set through competitive bidding. Pierre-Paul Schweitzer, head of the International Monetary Fund, warned that the United States was risking deeper balance of payments deficits because of overrapid domestic growth. New England Telephone Co. sold $100 million in bonds at a net interest cost of 6.13%, the highest price paid for financing by a Bell system unit since 1921.

The news in October was even worse. Profits of some large corporations, including General Electric, Alcoa, and Bethlehem Steel, didn't match the year-earlier figures in the third quarter.

Ford settled with the UAW, but the price tag was a (then) steep 6% a year for three years. The pact raised the prospect of similar or higher settlements in the steel, aerospace, and aluminum labor talks that were scheduled for 1968.

Meantime, domestic and international strife heightened. A major peace demonstration was held in Washington the weekend of October 21–22, and a jittery federal government called out troops to make sure the crowds didn't get out of hand. The following Monday, an Egyptian missile sank an Israeli destroyer in the Mediterranean Sea, killing 54 crewmen. Israel retaliated a few days later by shelling Egyptian oil refineries across the Suez. It was a pattern that was to be repeated for the remainder of the decade and into the 1970s.

The Downturn of 1969–70

This decline was the longest and most severe of the post-World War II years. In retrospect, it is remarkable that it didn't begin sooner.

In early April 1969, when we began our analysis, all of the factors that had led to the previous two downturns had worsened appreciably. On the economic front, bank interest rates had soared to around 7.5%. If labor was considered scarce when the unemployment rate stood at around 4%, it was downright rare at 3.5%. Living costs weren't just rising; they were skyrocketing. The major statistical indicators of the economy were in disarray.

American troop strength in Vietnam had leveled off but the antiwar protests hadn't. Outright student takeovers of major universities were becoming commonplace. The Israelis and the Arabs were sniping at each other across their borders, and another outbreak of hostilities seemed imminent. There was even a new development in crime—the airline hijacking.

Again, things weren't entirely grim. Some large companies were reporting higher first-quarter profits; General Motors' net for the period rose by a hefty 25%. On April 13, President Nixon presented Congress with a proposed budget that called for a surplus of $5.8 billion. GNP in the first three months of the year

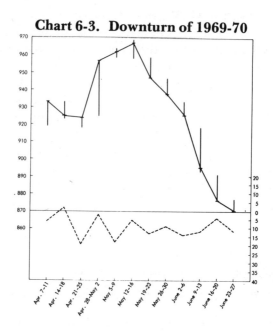

Chart 6-3. Downturn of 1969-70

rose by almost 2% to a record annual pace of more than $900 billion.

Such news, however, became rarer as April wore on. On April 21, the President asked for repeal of the 7% investment tax credit in an effort to cool the economy, upsetting many businessmen. The next day it was announced that factory orders in March had slumped by more than 4%. The *next* day the Consumer Price Index was released showing that prices in March alone had climbed by 0.9%, the largest monthly increase in 18 years.

The DJIA held its ground in the first three weeks of April despite the bad news, and the experts again were hard pressed to explain why. "The market's success in digesting so well a rather extensive menu of bearish items during the past several weeks constitutes favorable evidence of its physical stamina," said one analyst in "Abreast of the Market" on April 28, when the average stood at 924.

The next week was even more puzzling. French President Charles de Gaulle resigned, building contracts fell, and bank reserves shrank as credit reached its tightest state in almost two decades; yet the DJIA shot upward by 33 points.

The feature story of the May 1 *Wall Street Journal* was titled "Market Mystery," and the headline underneath read, "Stock Prices Head Up, And No One Is Certain What the Reasons Are." Some analysts quoted in the story had their theories. "The market got to the point where it paid no attention" to seemingly bad news and the arguments of the bears became so shopworn that they didn't have much effect, said Wall Street veteran Lucien O. Hooper of W. E. Hutton. Others gave the credit to the apparently improved climate surrounding the Vietnam peace talks in Paris.

Whatever their reasons, the analysts were decidedly bullish. Several predicted that the DJIA would top 1,000 shortly and even the 1,100 level was mentioned. The gloomiest bear who was quoted in the article looked for a decline to the area of 830 to 850. "One thing that seems clear . . . is that there is new support under the market," wrote the *Journal*'s reporter. "The big funds and institutions, which had been letting cash pile up, have returned to the market in a big way."

Any cheering effects that such a revelation might have was short-lived. Shortly thereafter, it was announced that unit labor costs in the first quarter took their sharpest increase in 13 years. The prime rate was under pressure to rise again. Purchasing agents noted an order slowdown in April and said it might signal a general downturn. In a May 7 front-pager, the *Journal* noted the discrepancies in the movement of the leading indicators and reached the same conclusion.

The market hit its peak of 969 on May 14, the day that the president was to give an evening television address. A dramatic new Vietnam peace move was expected, but it didn't come; Mr. Nixon merely renewed his call for mutual troop withdrawals. The market went into its slide. It was helped on its way down by more discouraging news. On the 16th it was announced that the first-quarter U.S. balance of payments deficit was the worst in two decades. On the 19th, corporate profits in the first quarter posted their slimmest overall gain in two years. On the 22nd, consumer prices rose 0.6% in April, a faster rate than had been expected.

The crusher came on June 9, when the nation's leading banks raised their prime rate of interest to 8.5%. It was the first full-point boost in the rate since 1945, sending the key figure to its then- modern-day peak. It erased any lingering doubts about the seriousness of the money crisis. Between June 9 and 12, the DJIA plunged by 32 points.

Once the decline had taken hold, even the sort of good news that was yearned for previously had little impact. For instance, President Nixon's June 8 announcement of a major U.S. troop withdrawal from Vietnam was swamped by the tide of concern over galloping inflation and tight money.

Unlike the previous two declines, the mid-1969 downturn of stock prices foreshadowed the general economic decline that was to come. By the fourth quarter of the year the economy was declared to be in recession.

The Downturn of 1971

The pattern of the market reversal of 1971 was quite different from that of the previous two. The news leading up to the April 28 peak was mostly good and it even stayed that way for the week of the turn itself. Once that point had been passed, however, negative news developments took over with a vengeance and carried the market down.

In late March of the year, when we picked up our analysis of the news, the economy was coming out of the recession of the previous year. The index of leading indicators had turned upward in the fourth quarter of 1970 and was moving ahead well, although some components lagged. Profits were advancing nicely and interest rates had declined by three points from their peak of two years before. Even the international scene seemed more benign. In late March, a U.S. Ping-Pong team was touring Red China, marking the first substantial break in more than 20 years of deep hostility between the two countries and signaling a possible way out of the Vietnam impasse.

The news in late March and early April reflected these developments. The banks cut their prime rate of interest to 5¼% from 5½%. The University of Michigan's quarterly survey showed that

Chart 6-4. Downturn of 1971

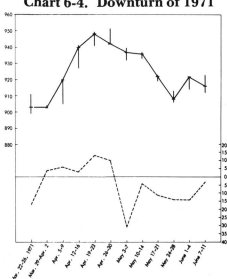

consumer confidence was strengthening. New car sales were posting good gains over 1970 periods. Even price boosts seemed to be moderating; March's wholesale price gain of 0.3% was half of February's increase, and consumer retail prices rose just 0.2% for the month.

The market responded strongly, gaining almost 20 points in the first week of April, 20 more in the second week, and 7 more in the third. The latter gain came despite the fact that the prime rate bounced back to 5½% on April 22.

The stock market's advance from its May 26, 1970 low of 631 was one of the swiftest in history, and the experts saw no quick end to it. On April 21, a front-page story in the *Journal* said that analysts were "practically unanimous" in the view that the DJIA would break through the 1,000 mark by year-end or sooner, barring any dramatic international or political setback. Some analysts expressed concern over the velocity of the market's advance and looked for a "correction" of 4% to 7%, but they were outnumbered by the optimists.

Most analysts weren't even worried about the fact that the up-turn in the economy still wasn't full-fledged. Robert T. Allen, research director at Shearson-Hammill, voiced the majority view in a *Journal* story. "The market has done what it's done without a whole lot of fuel from the economic statistics; it's been rising mostly on hopes and expectations," he said. "I think there's going to be enough economic fuel over the next two or three months to get to 1,000."

The market peaked at 951 on April 28, a Wednesday, losing 10 points to profit-taking before the week was out. Then, as May arrived, so did the bad news. The week of May 3–7 witnessed the following developments: An announcement that factory orders dropped in March for the first time in five months; a new likeli-hood of steel price increases; a dip in March construction spending; and an admission by Treasury Secretary Shultz that the federal budget deficit in the fiscal year ending June 30 would be "noticeably larger" than the $18.6 billion that was originally forecast.

Worst of all, a world monetary crisis erupted with West Ger-many's announcement on May 5 that it would no longer support the dollar at current levels. The development jolted investors into closer inspection of some trends that had gone all but unnoticed as stocks surged upward. These included the continuing outflow of dollars (caused in part by foreign interest rates higher than those in the United States) and inflation at home, fueled by federal budget deficits and the stepped-up growth in the money supply. World monetary uncertainty in itself has long been considered bad for the market, and some of the remedies that might be applied to rectify things—limits on foreign investment, tighter credit, and other measures to slow domestic economic growth—seemed no more palatable. The monetary mess was to dog the market for some months, overshadowing such few favorable devel-opments as the mid-May announcement that corporate profits grew by a hefty 13% in the first quarter.

There was other bad news as the market went into decline. The week of May 17, a nationwide railroad strike hit, short-term interest rates rose sharply, and orders for machine tools and durable goods declined. The following week it was announced that the United States had a foreign trade deficit in April, the first unfavorable balance since February 1969. The major aluminum companies concluded labor negotiations by awarding the United Steelworkers a three-year contract with a 31% increase and then immediately raised prices by 6%. An angry Administration called the moves inflationary.

Abroad, the Communists were launching new attacks in Vietnam and Laos, and Egypt and Russia signed a 15-year military assistance pact, making a Middle East peace settlement seem even more distant. The stock price decline would be no mere correction.

7

The Market
and the News in 1972

STOCK market historians will remember 1972 as the
year the Dow Jones Industrial Average first closed above 1,000. It
happened late in the year, when it appeared that the United States
at long last would be getting out of Vietnam. Peace didn't actually
come until January 1973, at which time the market went down.
But that's another story.

The market gained 14.6% from the beginning of 1972 to the
end, which is about three times the average annual increase of the
previous 45 years. That gain, however, was achieved wholly in the
first three months and the last two months. When the year began,
the market was in the process of rebounding from its low of 790 in
November 1971. The Dow opened at 889 and moved up to the 970
level in April before beginning seven months of wavering within a
60-point range. In November the market resumed its climb,
reaching a high of 1,036 before closing the year at 1,020.

Economically, 1972 was a year of continued recovery from the 1969–70 recession. Economists had called the recession mild, so many people were surprised by the sputtering, halting convalescence. By 1972, most economic indicators were proclaiming advances, but many investors, especially little guys who had suffered losses in the steep 1969 downturn, seemed skeptical that the gains could be sustained.

There was justification for this skepticism. In 1971, rampant inflation, induced largely by the Vietnam war, caused President Nixon first to declare a wage-price freeze, called Phase 1, and then late that year to institute a system of wage-price controls, called Phase 2. These controls were to last throughout 1972. On the whole, they seemed to slow down inflation somewhat—except for the price of food, because raw farm products weren't regulated. But it took most of the year for Phase 2 to make its modest achievements apparent. Meanwhile, there were worries that Phase 2 wouldn't work and inflation would continue, or that Phase 2 might stymie what still looked like a fragile business recovery and plunge the economy into another recession.

Otherwise, Vietnam was the news with the most direct and obvious influence on the market. Whenever progress seemed to be made toward peace, the market went up. Whenever something happened to impede United States withdrawal, the market went down.

The issues of the economy and the war created a great deal of uncertainty during the middle half of the year. Not until the final two months were both issues in a positive trend, and that's when the market shot up.

The news was mostly good during the year, with 56% of the days and 69% of the weeks registering positive on the News Index. Table 7-A shows the breakdown. The bad news was fairly well distributed throughout the year; the longest stretch that the index remained negative was three weeks in late March and early April. However, in late June and again in mid-July there was some decidedly bad news that tilted the News Index mostly negative for an eight-week period from late May through the third week in July. For the rest of the year, however, the News Index was positive, with the most intense good news coming from late October through mid-November, when the DJIA posted its most dramatic gains (see Chart 7-1).

Chart 7-1. News and the Market in 1972

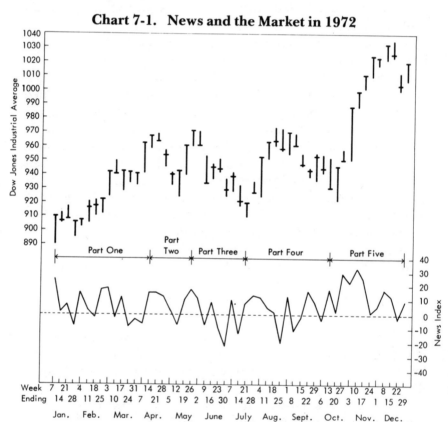

Table 7-A.   1972 News Summary

Period	Positive	Negative	Zero
Days	140	99	12
Weeks	36	16	0

For purposes of detailed analysis, we divided the year into five periods, corresponding to what we identified as distinct phases of the market. In four of these periods the news and the market moved in the same direction most of the time—that is, in weeks that the news was positive the market went up, and in weeks the news was negative the market went down. Overall, the news and the market moved in the same direction 77% of the year on a weekly basis, and in opposite directions 23% (see Table 7-B).

Table 7-B. Movement of the News Index and the Market

	Weeks in Same Direction	Weeks in Opposite Direction
Period 1	13	2
Period 2	2	4
Period 3	6	2
Period 4	10	2
Period 5	9	2
Total	40	12

Period 1: January 3–April 14

In the first 15 weeks of 1972, the market climbed 79 points from 889 to 968—a 9% gain. The news was positive roughly 60% of the time, as shown in the breakdown in Table 7-C.

Generally, this was a time of good economic news and bad

Table 7-C. Period 1 News Summary

Period	Positive	Negative	Zero
Days	41	31	2
Weeks	9	6	0

Vietnam news. Interest rates were falling in the first part of 1972, and corporate earnings were rising. Other indicators were on the upswing, too, though not steadily and not in unison. The bad economic news, such as a dock strike and predictions of a bigger federal budget deficit, came only sporadically and in small amounts.

But news about Vietnam went from bad to worse. In January, President Nixon said on national television that Hanoi was ignoring his latest peace offer. In February, the United States stepped up its bombing raids. In early March, the United States walked out of the Paris peace talks, precipitating what the press called the worst crisis in the three years of the negotiations. In early April, North Vietnam began a major offensive in the south, overrunning several Allied bases. President Nixon responded by resuming massive bombing of North Vietnam for the first time in 42 months.

The good economic news prevailed, however. Perhaps one reason is that the bad news from Vietnam was countered by President Nixon's visit to the People's Republic of China in February. Not only did the visit augur well for reduced international tensions, but it seemed to imply that the Vietnam conflict might be settled sooner rather than later.

Only twice did the news and the market go in opposite directions. In the second week of January the market fell 4 points while the news continued positive. There were no major news items during this period to account for the divergence, but there was an interesting anomaly in the news flow that week—of the 33 items that received a positive or negative score, 18 of them were negative and only 15 positive. The News Index didn't reflect this because there were more positive items above the *Journal's* horizontal fold, where they accumulated more points, than negative items. The overall tone of the news, however, was negative.

The News Index and the market also parted company in the first week of April. This time the market gained 22 points, but the News Index was negative, reflecting the start of the North Vietnamese offensive and the massive U.S. bombing in retaliation. The economic news during this week was very good—the first reports of higher first-quarter earnings, an increase in auto sales, and a report from the University of Michigan that consumers' expectations about business conditions and employment were showing "substantial improvement." Even though the News Index was negative for the week, as a result of bad Vietnam news dominating the high-point items, the total items were evenly divided between positive and negative.

This was one of the few times all year that good economic news and bad Vietnam news met head-on during a single week. That the market chose to react primarily to the good economic news probably comes as no surprise to seasoned market observers. Economic news usually has the most basic influence on the market, especially when conditions are such that good economic news has the effect of easing uncertainties about the future. In such times, only tremendous, jolting calamities overseas could exert greater market influence, and in those early weeks of 1972 the Vietnam war had been dragging on for so long that it lacked that kind of punch.

Period 2: April 17–May 26

In this period, the news and the market moved in opposite directions two-thirds of the time. The market dropped 26 points in three weeks and then rebounded 30 points in the following three weeks, while the news flowed positive for five out of the six weeks. Table 7-D gives the breakdown.

Table 7-D.   Period 2 News Summary

Period	Positive	Negative	Zero
Days	18	10	2
Weeks	5	1	0

Good economic news kept the News Index positive in the first three weeks, but there was a difference—a lot of it was repetitive reports of higher corporate earnings and other economic advances made during the first quarter. These items served to confirm investors' expectations, but they were no longer exciting in themselves.

Moreover, the bad economic news—there were five negative days to ten positive days in the first half of this period—was unsettling. Phase 2 controllers said they had been looking at first-quarter profits, too, and were preparing to order "hundreds of millions of dollars" in price reductions; the prime rate began edging up, reaching 5¼%; steel shipments began to look less robust to some producers, and several steelmakers reported lower first-quarter earnings; and wholesale prices were rising fast, the government reported.

The Vietnam war became more chilling, too. U.S. bombers struck Hanoi and the port of Haiphong in North Vietnam, and the North Vietnamese threatened "all-out war." The bombing was then curtailed, but North Vietnamese troops continued their offensive in the south.

The news turned negative in the fourth week, when President Nixon ordered a blockade of North Vietnamese harbors to cut off Soviet and Chinese shipments of war materiel. That was announced the evening of May 8; the following day the market sank 13 points. Continuing coverage of the blockade kept the index negative for the week, but the market started moving up on Wednesday, in part because the blockade didn't seem to be scuttling President Nixon's planned summit trip to Moscow later in the month. "If the summit meeting is on, we have to assume there won't be any U.S.-Russian confrontation," one broker observed in the *Journal*'s "Abreast of the Market" column on May 11.

In the next two weeks, the news resumed its positive flow as the market rebounded. The unsettling economic news was replaced with items of a more reassuring nature: The government reported improved industrial production and higher personal income, suggesting that the economic recovery was accelerating; it appeared that Phase 2 was beginning to moderate the rate of inflation; and the index of leading indicators advanced strongly. From Moscow came several positive items regarding the cordial talks and important agreements between President Nixon and Secretary Brezhnev. These signaled a general thawing in relations that even escalation of the Vietnam war didn't disrupt.

Straightforward, objective analysis of the news in this period simply wasn't adequate to emphasize the items the market considered important. Routine economic items racked up all the points in the first half, effectively drowning out the unsettling news. In the second half, the good economic news was more forward-looking. Also, the bad news about Vietnam wasn't given a chance to linger and cause doubts. Neither the Russians nor the Chinese reacted very strongly to the blockade of North Vietnam and the Moscow summit came off as scheduled, so investors' worst fears were eased within a few days.

Period 3: May 30–July 21

This is the only distinctly declining period for the market in 1972, and the news was negative. In eight weeks the market dropped from 971 to 920, while the News Index registered negative 64% of the days but only 50% of the weeks, as shown in Table 7-E.

Table 7-E.　Period 3 News Summary

Period	Positive	Negative	Zero
Days	13	23	0
Weeks	4	4	0

As the discrepancy between the days and the weeks indicates, this was a period of alternating waves of good news and bad news, virtually all of it on the economic front. This played into investors' uncertainties about the future of the economy, as did the major noneconomic news of this period—George McGovern clinching the Democratic nomination for president on a platform that at one point called for massive tax reform (i.e., higher taxes for business and capital gains investors) and cash grants to the needy.

The economic news was predominantly bad in this period. Wholesale and retail prices and interest rates continued rising and unemployment remained high; gold prices began soaring in foreign markets, which signaled the possibility of another international monetary trauma and was followed by the British pound being allowed to float. The leading indicators slowed from their previous rate of gain, and mutual fund redemptions continued to exceed sales. The good economic news, mainly such things as higher auto sales and gains in a few minor indicators, dominated in some weeks, but it simply wasn't as important as the bad news.

Such was the case in the first week of this period, shortened by Memorial Day, when the News Index was positive but the market dropped 10 points. The index was buoyed by such items as a report of a 6% surge in construction contracts and the windup of the successful summit meeting in Moscow. But the major items above the fold were slightly negative, seven items to six. Among them were reports of a 22% decline in machine tool orders, a widening foreign trade deficit, and an apparent tightening of credit by the Federal Reserve Board—the kind of news that underscored the uncertainty about future economic gains.

The news and the market also moved in opposite directions during the final week of this period, with the market easing 2 points while the New Index was positive. Again, the good news was bloated by a run of routine items, in this case favorable earnings reports for the June 30 quarter. Nearly 60% of all the items graded that week were positive, but above the fold the good and bad items were evenly divided. And again, the bad news was unsettling: a snag developed in the steel industry's recovery; price reductions were ordered by the Phase 2 controllers; extensive damage in the East was caused by Tropical Storm Agnes; and industrial output rose at an unexpectedly sluggish rate in June.

Period 4: July 24–October 13

This is the longest period of marking time in 1972. In these twelve weeks the Dow rose from 935˙to 974 and then sagged back to 930. The news was positive about two-thirds of the time, as shown in Table 7-F, but some sharp seesawing from positive to

Table 7-F. Period 4 News Summary

Period	Positive	Negative	Zero
Days	36	19	3
Weeks	8	4	0

negative in the middle of this period seemed to reflect the lack of any conclusive developments that would have put the market on a more decisive course. It was no coincidence that the period of instability in the News Index was occurring when the market rally ran out of steam.

Up to that point the news was positive and the market rose steadily. While the Vietnam war droned on in the background, the news was dominated by economic tidings such as these: a report of the sharpest rise in GNP since 1965; a surge in durable goods orders; earnings and production rising at the auto makers.

The bad news took hold in the fifth week of this period when the News Index plunged sharply negative and the market fell more than 6 points. The market climbed the first two days of the week as President Nixon was renominated for a second term. But then it lost 15 points in two days on such news as higher interest rates, worsening inflation, and sharp limitations imposed by price controllers on price boosts for 1973 model autos.

The market rebounded on positive news in the next week, but in the following two weeks the news turned negative and the market lost ground. The News Index's jitters seemed to infect investors with uncertainty and to nip the market's rally; market-trading volume slumped at this point, too.

The News Index turned positive in the ninth week but the market continued to fall—one of only two weeks that the news and the market went in opposite directions during this period. Typically, the good news consisted mainly of reheated developments, such as a continued rise in housing starts and a jump in industrial output. The feelings of uncertainty, meanwhile, were fueled by tensions in the Mideast and in Vietnam and by another rise in mutual fund redemptions coupled with a decline in sales.

The economic news continued routinely positive the following week, but the market rallied on hopes of a peace agreement in Vietnam—the first of several such rallies in the second half of 1972. Henry Kissinger and North Vietnam's Le Duc Tho were conducting what were described as "intense" talks in Paris. But it became evident the next week that a Vietnam peace wasn't imminent, and that, in addition to bad economic news, such as more rises in the prime interest rate and wholesale prices, caused the market to fall.

Peace hopes resurfaced in the final week of this period as Dr. Kissinger and Le Duc Tho resumed their talks. This moved the market up on Monday and Tuesday, but then the talks ended with no agreement, leaving the market with a hangover from its peace-hope euphoria. In such a mood, investors paid little attention to the good economic news but, according to brokers, reacted instead to a prediction of still higher interest rates. This was the second week of diverse moves in the News Index and the market, which clearly was disappointed by the elusive peace.

Period 5: October 16–December 29

This is the period when good economic news and solid peace developments combined to push the DJIA from 922 to well over 1,000. The news was positive in 62% of the days and 91% of the weeks, as shown in Table 7-G.

Table 7-G.   Period 5 News Summary

Period	Positive	Negative	Zero
Days	32	15	5
Weeks	10	1	0

The peace news began in the middle of the first week of this period when Dr. Kissinger left the Paris talks for a surprise trip to Saigon. When he returned to the United States neither he nor President Nixon said anything until Hanoi announced that a pact had been agreed upon. Dr. Kissinger held a press conference on October 26 and announced, "Peace is at hand." As it turned out, that hand had a long reach, but it was theretofore the clearest indication that the United States would finally extricate itself from the economically and socially disastrous Vietnam conflict. The elated market soared, and volume picked up sharply, too.

Economic news was very positive through Thanksgiving. A barrage of strong third-quarter earnings reports and announcement of a big trade agreement with the Soviet Union were prominent in the first couple of weeks. They completely overwhelmed more ominous bad news, such as the first signs of more international currency upheavals, an accelerating gain in the consumer price index, and a widening of the U.S. trade deficit—all of which came home to roost early in 1973.

The Dow Jones Industrial Average closed at 1,003 on November 14, the first time the market ended a day above that bench mark. By the time it got there, it was becoming evident that peace wasn't as close as Dr. Kissinger had implied. But the market was sustained by a flow of good economic news that allowed only three negative days on the News Index in four weeks. Some of the news was surprisingly good: unexpected increases in economic indicators, including GNP; and a *Wall Street Journal* survey of businessmen who said they looked for corporate profits to rise by more than 13% in 1973. The market seemed unruffled by another prime rate boost.

The week after Thanksgiving, however, the market sagged while the News Index held positive. Brokers wrote off the small decline as an encouragingly mild "consolidation" following the strong rise. Vague but growing disappointment about the lack of a peace settlement also was cited. About the only economic news worth noting was bad: The government revised its leading indicators index for September from a 0.4% advance to a 0.2% decline.

The market rebounded the next week on news that the secret Paris peace talks were under way again. But the market sank 6 points the second week in December, while the News Index remained positive. Again, brokers pronounced the decline a consolidation phase. "In such a classic pullback," said one analyst in "Abreast of the Market" on December 13, "the Dow Jones Industrial Average could drop to 1,000 without breaking its basic upward thrust."

And that's exactly what it did the following week, the only week of negative news during this period. The Paris peace talks hit a serious snag, and President Nixon ordered resumption of full-scale bombing of North Vietnam. News of yet another prime rate boost in the offing also helped depress things.

The year ended on the upswing for both the market and the News Index. Bombing of North Vietnam resumed after a Christmas lull and a higher prime rate was posted by several banks, but both developments had been anticipated in earlier news stories. Heavy year-end tax trading also influenced the market.

Summary and Conclusions

The first test of our News Index was to apply it to the major upturns and downturns of the six years preceding 1972. We found that after each peak or valley had been reached, the news and the market moved in the same direction, indicating that stocks can't continue to fall in the face of a sustained dose of good news, nor continue to rise when the news is decisively bad.

Equally important is what the findings don't show—that it is not always possible to pick a market top or bottom, except in retrospect, by examining the news. As we structured it, the News Index seems to be a concurrent indicator of market movements.

This came through again when we measured the news flow throughout 1972. We found that the news and stocks moved in the same direction nearly 80% of the time, including the periods of decisive market movement.

It also was apparent that there is some art involved in interpreting the news. Times when the market didn't react predictably to news, or failed to react at all, suggests that individual news developments might be viewed as part of a total context, or national mood. Subjective insights that supplement the News Index undoubtedly help illuminate current market trends.

The news can be observed in ways other than on a broad-scale daily or weekly basis. One way is to concentrate on major news issues. In the next three chapters we analyze three of these, shifting to a qualitative evaluation of the news.

Part III

Issues and Stocks

8

The War in Vietnam:
When Good News Turns Bad

THERE are some events that influence the market and the flow of the news over long periods of time. War is one of them.

Is war good for the economy and the stock market, or bad? There is no simple answer to this question, which is why the prospect of war always causes some trepidation among investors.

Karl Marx contended that capitalist nations needed and purposely spawned wars to keep their production lines rolling. There are devout anti-communists who also equate war with economic growth, higher profits, and higher stock prices.

The position is not without justification. Wars cost money—lots of it. World War I cost the United States $31.6 billion, World War II $315.2 billion, and the Korean conflict $79.1 billion. The national bill for the war in Vietnam came to more than $135 billion.

To be sure, a lot of this money was spent overseas, never to return. But much of it rippled through the U.S. economy. The defense industry is one of the largest employers in the country. Counting wives, children, and other dependents of civilian defense workers, an estimated 15% to 20% of the nation's population is dependent upon defense work for their financial support. Moreover, at least some of the workers in virtually every other sector of the economy also owe their jobs to military spending, according to labor analysts.

Profits and economic stimuli aren't the only reasons that some stock market experts think that war is bullish. "The reason for buying stocks on war or fear of war is not that war, in itself, is ever again likely to be profitable to American stockholders. It is just that money becomes even less desirable, so that stock prices, which are expressed in units of money, always go up," wrote investment counselor Philip A. Fisher. "In other words, war is always bearish on money. To sell stock at the threatened or actual outbreak of hostilities so as to get into cash is extreme financial lunacy."[1]

The contrary view is that peace is most beneficial to the economy because war can cause such undesirable side effects such as inflation, federal budget and international payments deficits, and wage-price controls. Investors holding this view would tend to react negatively to escalation of a conflict and positively to conciliation and moves toward peace.

Recent history gives a mixed reading on which theory holds the most water. At the outset of war, the peace theory seems most valid because stock prices slumped with the outbreak of World Wars I and II and the Korean conflict. There was no precise starting date for the Vietnam war, but brief market reversals in both 1964 and early 1965 coincided with news of developing crisis in Southeast Asia. "Furthermore," Mr. Fisher pointed out, "at least ten times in the last twenty-two years, news has come of other international crises which gave threat of major war. In every instance, stocks dipped sharply on the fear of war and rebounded sharply as the war scare subsided." So much for Wall Street capitalists thirsting after war.

But once the war is underway and it becomes apparent that it will not worsen, the market typically rallies. During World War I, for instance, the market began climbing early in 1915, and by September 1916 the Dow Jones Industrial Average had doubled. The market also moved up substantially in 1943–45 and from mid-1950 to late 1951. As already indicated, the market staged four major upswings during the course of the Vietnam war. In all these wars, the economic gains resulting in part from the military spending were the major impetus in pushing the market up.

Even so, the market likes to anticipate peace, too. In every war in this century, the market has rallied strongly in the final months of conflict on news of coming peace. But when peace actually arrived, the market usually slumped—probably a classic example of the discounting of a widely anticipated event. The only exception was World War II, when the bull market that began in the spring of 1945 continued into the summer of 1946 before faltering. After most wars, the peace slump was only temporary and the market began climbing thereafter (see Chart 8-1).

Chart 8-1. Impact on Stocks When a War Ends: The Fate of $1,000 Invested in the Dow Jones Industrials

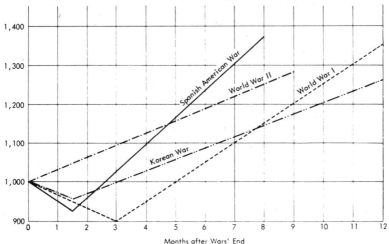

Months after Wars' End

Source: Ralph A. Rotnem, *Market Review*, Harris, Upham & Company, Inc.

We will attempt to sort out the interplay between war news and the market in the context of the Vietnam war, which raged for eight years and precipitated some far-reaching economic and social changes in the United States. We chose this war because it is the most recent one involving U.S. forces and because it seems reasonable to assume that any future market-affecting conflict this country may enter will be similar to it. In this age of nuclear weapons, discussion of the stock market implications of a World War II-type confrontation would border on the ridiculous.

It is, of course, fallacious to ascribe every move of the market to a single issue, even one as important as war, when it is obvious that stock prices are influenced by a wide variety of factors. That's why it is impossible to quantify the influence of war news in the same way that we measured the flow of the news in previous chapters. Instead, we must use a broad-brush approach, which admittedly isn't precise but still affords some insights.

The Buildup

U.S. military advisers were first sent to Vietnam in 1961, but it wasn't until the latter part of 1964 that the Indochina situation began sounding like a war to most Americans. In August of that year, North Vietnamese patrol boats attacked two U.S. naval ships in the Gulf of Tonkin. President Johnson retaliated by ordering the first air bombings of North Vietnam, and Congress passed a resolution authorizing the president "to take all necessary measures to repel any armed attack against the forces of the United States and to prevent further aggression." During the week of this crisis, the market dipped about 25 points.

By May 1965, President Johnson had authorized that more than 50,000 U.S. troops be sent to Vietnam to support South Vietnamese forces that were faced with an attack. A month later he authorized U.S. troops to be used in combat, and by July there were 125,000 American soldiers in Vietnam. The United States was at war.

From Wall Street's point of view, the growing Vietnam conflict initially looked like a limited war in a far-off land with few broad implications for the U.S. economy. The generals said they could use sophisticated technology to beat down the ragtag Communists from the north. It probably would all be over in a year or so, but meanwhile it was just the ticket to get a little more mileage out of a bull market that had begun in 1962 and had already gained 70% by early 1965.

What many investors perceived as an economy threatening to go sluggish turned out to be a natural and orderly deceleration of an amazing economic boom. By the time the Vietnam buildup reached meaningful proportions, business was operating at a hotter pace than when the Korean conflict began in 1950—industry was operating at 90% of capacity (versus 80% at the onset of the Korean war), and the unemployment rate was a tight 4.5% (versus 5.4%). These factors quickly came into play as the government found that in many instances it had to force industry to bid on war contracts. In early 1966, a *Wall Street Journal* survey of a wide range of industries showed that war-caused delays clearly were beginning to pinch some civilian customers. The survey suggested that a further expansion of the conflict would put a quick end to any ideas that the U.S. economy was big enough to also supply a burgeoning civilian market without trouble.[2]

But in 1965 more meant better, and investors bid up stock prices in happy anticipation of fat defense contracts. Table 8-A shows how various stock groups performed in comparison to the market from June 24, 1965—which was just a few days before the market hit its low point of the year of 841—to February 10, 1966 —which was just one day after the market closed at its then record level of 995. The table also shows how these stocks performed from February 10 to March 17, which was the first month of a bear market that dipped to 744 on October 7 of that year.

Of the sixteen stock groups that outperformed the DJIA on the upside, nine were directly influenced by the expanding Vietnam war. Aircraft manufacturers, already humming with civilian jet orders, geared up to produce military planes, too. Airlines boosted earnings sharply by carrying troops and supplies to Vietnam because the military didn't have enough transport planes of its own. Electrical equipment, heavy machinery, machine tools, and nonferrous metals (especially copper) all benefited from the

Table 8-A.   Stock Group Performance

	June 24, 1965	% Change June 24 to Feb. 10	% Change Feb. 10 to March 17
DJ Ind. Avg.	857.76	+ 15.5	− 7.21
DJ Rails Avg.	191.79	+ 38.6	− 7.1
DJ Utils Avg.	153.09	− 3.4	− 3.5
Aircraft Mfg.	172.11	+ 137.1	− 16.9
Air Transport	179.78	+ 47.1	− 6.0
Auto Mfg.	166.92	+ 15.6	− 6.9
Auto Equip.	115.59	+ 14.7	− 7.9
Banks	167.98	+ 3.6	− 9.8
Bldg Mtrls.	184.98	+ 2.4	− 7.7
Chemicals	380.88	+ 4.0	− 4.7
Drugs	467.81	+ 26.0	− 6.3
Electrical Equip.	397.22	+ 26.3	− 5.0
Farm Equip.	273.50	+ 50.8	− 8.6
Foods, Bvgs.	228.00	+ 6.0	− 4.2
Gold Mining	85.30	+ 27.1	− 4.1
Grocery Chains	319.83	− 16.7	− 6.4
Installment Fin.	211.16	+ 0.4	− 8.6
Insurance	706.61	+ 3.3	− 9.7
Machine Tools	64.32	+ 50.9	− 8.5
Machinery (Hvy.)	52.88	+ 35.1	− 1.0
Motion Pictures	87.90	+ 23.7	− 2.1
Nonferrous Mtls.	107.37	+ 44.4	− 3.3
Office Equip.	1102.79	+ 15.1	− 2.9
Oil	327.44	+ 4.6	− 7.7
Packing (Meat)	37.22	+ 23.3	− 1.3
Paper	133.89	+ 13.7	− 3.5
RR Equip.	81.73	+ 36.8	− 10.6
Retail Merch.	468.23	− 8.1	− 6.0
Rubber	407.06	+ 3.6	− 7.5
Steel, Iron	253.38	+ 11.5	− 8.0
Television	192.54	+ 107.3	− 4.7
Textiles	277.39	+ 46.0	− 10.3
Tobacco	117.41	+ 9.9	− 2.2

Source: *Wall Street Journal*, March 21, 1966. The stock group averages were compiled by *Barron's Financial Weekly*.

start-up of war production. Railroads also carried material bound for war, and as the rail stocks advanced so did those of rail equipment makers. Textile manufacturers, busy with civilian demand, had to stretch their capacity to the limit to outfit a growing number of soldiers.

Five of those nine upside gainers also resisted the market's decline through March 17. Those that didn't, analysts said, were especially vulnerable to profit-taking. In the case of textiles, there was some worry that the war would necessitate a tax increase, which would leave consumers with less money to spend on clothing.

Peace prospects, meanwhile, were bearish. Several times in 1965 and early 1966 the market broke on news of peace feelers or other diplomatic actions that might bring the war to an early end. Peace news didn't have a lingering influence on the market in those days, but it did cause some daily gyrations. Typical was the market of December 29, 1965, as described in "Abreast of the Market" the following morning:

> "Everybody's trying to second-guess the Vietnam situation" [one broker said]. Defense stocks were weak early in the session, as they had been earlier this week, because of the belief that the recent peace maneuverings might result in a permanent cease-fire in Southeast Asia. This uncertainty also influenced the rest of the market, brokers asserted.
>
> Yesterday afternoon news came that President Ho Chi Minh of North Vietnam said his conditions for peace talks include the withdrawal of U.S. troops from South Vietnam. He added that "U.S. leaders want war and not peace." This statement sent the defense issues bounding upward. But a later pullback in prices followed news that U.S. Ambassador to the UN Arthur J. Goldberg called on Pope Paul VI on a special mission from President Johnson to talk about Vietnam.

Perhaps the one caveat that Wall Street had about the expanding war was how President Johnson planned to pay for it. Would it be through tax increases, reduced spending in other areas, or what? In a study of stock market reaction to Vietnam and

Korean war news, Betty C. Hanson and Bruce M. Russett describe the effect of this concern on the market.

In July of 1965 the market declined on several occasions, according to analysts, because of rumors that the economy was about to be put on a war-type footing with wage and price controls and an excess-profits tax instituted. However, when President Johnson finally made his statement on forthcoming war measures, he called for *only* doubling of the draft, and consequently the market was said to rise out of relief that nothing worse was contemplated.[3]

President Johnson wanted both guns and butter, and said as much in his State of the Union message of January 12, 1966. A *Wall Street Journal* account the next morning noted: "The President rejected the argument of many Republicans and some Democrats that the Great Society should be curtailed to provide the funds for the Vietnam war. If they feel current Federal revenue is inadequate, he implied, they should raise taxes rather than attempt to hold down domestic spending."

Increased taxes did come eventually, but not enough and not in time to curtail a painful increase in inflation that continued until after U.S. participation in the war had ended.

Shifting Attitudes

Vietnam did not remain good news for very long, however. As the stock market declined during most of 1966, the economic news centered mostly on how the economy was overheating and inflation was speeding up. The market pulled out of its 250-point slump in October, but there was no reversing the changing attitude toward Vietnam that had been building throughout the year. By 1967, Vietnam had become bad news, and investors clearly wanted de-escalation.

In early February 1967, a Gallup Poll turned up a 52% negative response to this question: "In view of the developments since we entered the fighting in Vietnam, do you think the U.S. made a mistake sending troops to fight in Vietnam?" "No" answers dropped to 50% in May, 48% in July and 42% in October.

On May 16, 1967, the *Wall Street Journal* reported, "The consensus of 100 leading industrialists was that business will be further strained by the Vietnam war, shrinking profits, higher taxes, a ballooning federal budget deficit, more militant labor, and more skittish shoppers."

In Dodge City, Kansas, the mood had changed markedly, *Wall Street Journal* reporter Everett Groseclose found. He visited the community in 1966 and reported a ground swell of patriotic support for the war. But in mid-1967 sentiment had shifted to war weariness and deep-seated doubts. (He returned two more times. In 1969 Dodge was downright dovish, he wrote, and in 1972 its citizens expressed feelings of helplessness and frustration that were brought on by the war and that affected many aspects of their lives.)

This shift in attitude began to make waves in the stock market by early 1968. A front-page *Wall Street Journal* article entitled "Dovish Wall Street," published on March 6, 1968, described the reaction.

> The last time the market heard vague rumors that North Vietnam might be willing to talk peace, the Dow-Jones Industrials spurted 7.78 points in a single day, Jan. 8, to their recently closing peak of 908.92. When those rumors proved unfounded, prices began to drop, and the break accelerated sharply when ferocious Vietcong attacks erupted in cities throughout South Vietnam. By Feb. 13, the average had plunged 77.15 points, or 8.48%, to a close of 831.77. A minor recovery followed, but it gave way to a new decline as soon as reports circulated that the Administration was considering committing more troops to Vietnam and calling up some reserves; yesterday's close was a 14-month low.

At the end of March, President Johnson announced new peace initiatives, as well as his decision not to run for reelection, and the market shot up. Meanwhile, defense industries had fallen out of favor with investors. "Strange as it may seem, in view of the faster tempo of the war, there is a definite prejudice against stocks with a high national defense emphasis," noted Lucien O. Hooper of W. E. Hutton & Co.[4]

Winding Down

Richard Nixon was elected president in November 1968 in

part because he said he had a plan to end the Vietnam war and his opponent, Hubert Humphrey, was closely associated with the out-of-favor policies of the Johnson Administration. President Nixon's "plan" was to gradually withdraw U.S. troops and "Vietnamize" the war, while keeping up bombing pressure on the Communists and secretly entreating them to negotiate a peace settlement. In implementing this plan, he asserted that wage-price controls wouldn't be necessary to contain war-fueled inflation at home. By August 1971, it was clear they were needed, however, and he imposed a complete freeze. In late fall, Phase 2 of the controls was put into effect.

More than a half-million U.S. military men were in Vietnam when President Nixon ordered the first troop withdrawals in June 1969. In the next three years he withdrew all but about 40,000 troops, who remained until a peace settlement was made in January 1973.

The president began winding the war down in other ways, too. Defense expenditures declined from $78.7 billion in fiscal 1969 to $77.9 billion in fiscal 1970 and $75.5 billion in fiscal 1971. This drop in spending hit the aerospace industry especially hard because the National Aeronautics and Space Administration and civilian airlines also were cutting back.

"Aerospace employment has always fluctuated," the *Wall Street Journal* noted in a front-page article on May 15, 1970. "But economists say that now, for the first time since World War II, not only production workers but thousands of highly educated engineers and scientists are being laid off and this time they have no place to go."

By the beginning of 1971, the top-ranking defense contractor —Lockheed Aircraft Corp.—was teetering on the brink of bankruptcy and had to be bailed out with a government loan guarantee.

In the view of many analysts, the decline of the aerospace industry was an important factor contributing to the recession of 1969–70, which was accompanied by the worst bear market in many years. The market's few rallies during this period were almost invariably prompted by news of peace maneuverings. When peace failed to materialize, continuing bad economic news again dragged the market down.

Anticipating Peace

"Now the war on inflation and its many attendant evils, such as a credit crunch, economic slowdown, and profit squeeze, are nudging Vietnam into a lesser position of influence on the market's course," remarked stockbroker Eugene E. Peroni in the *Journal*'s "Abreast of the Market" column on June 5, 1969. "The war and very elusive peace still are powerful influences, and will continue to be, but their force will be felt only sporadically until finally there is tangible evidence of the ultimate achievement—formal peace."

Mr. Peroni's assessment remained accurate far longer than probably he or anybody else expected. Meanwhile, investors were curious about what peace would mean to the economy. The press catered to this interest with many stories, which tended to be published in clusters each time there seemed to be substantial movement toward peace.

The *Wall Street Journal* ran a few of these stories as early as 1966, but they didn't begin appearing with any regularity in the *Journal* or elsewhere until 1968, when the Paris peace talks began. At first, these stories dwelled on the tremendous economic "peace dividend" that assertedly would result from ending the war. Here are the first few paragraphs of a *Journal* story entitled "When the War Ends" that ran on July 5, 1968.

WASHINGTON—Once peace comes to Vietnam, look for quite a fight on the home front.

The stakes: Up to $30 billion a year in Federal spending that will be freed by the end of hostilities.

As peace comes to look less remote, the question of how to divide up the huge budgetary boon is beginning to look less pleasurable. The Pentagon is already starting to stake out claims for keeping a large chunk of its Vietnam money, and unless difficult decisions on peaceful uses for the remainder are swiftly adopted, Johnson Administration officials fear, the economy might lurch aimlessly from inflation into recession, as it did after Korea.

"When the war ends, we're going to face a hard choice on what to do with what's left over," says one Administration aide. Even then, warns Sherman J. Faisel of the Federal Reserve Board, "We will still have more demands than resources."

But wouldn't the defense sector of the economy suffer from peace? Not really, said another *Journal* story of the same period in reporting on a survey of defense contractors. "Military suppliers divide about evenly between those who expect an end to the war to hurt their sales and profits only mildly, during a transition period lasting perhaps six months to a year, and those who don't expect it to hurt at all." Many suppliers believe that "whatever military business is lost will be more than outweighed before long by a boom in the consumer economy and a speedup of Government programs, ranging from space exploration to water purification."

Moreover, the story went on, peace could boost some defense contractors' profit margins. "Defense business at many, though not all, companies is relatively low-profit work. For instance, the aerospace divisions of Textron Inc., including Bell Helicopter, accounted for more than 44% of Textron's 1967 sales of $1.4 billion but for less than 28% of Textron's 1967 profit of $117.1 million. William Miller, Textron president, estimates that a 20% post-Vietnam drop in defense sales—which he doesn't expect—could be compensated for, so far as its impact on profit, by a rise of only 10% in Textron's commercial sales."[5]

Besides buoying the market in general, peace news also boosted prices of certain groups of securities. These became known as "peace stocks," and stories were written about them, too. In the spring of 1969, for instance, when news of peace maneuverings was enough to rally the market and interrupt the beginning of the bear market, the *Journal*'s "Heard on the Street" column noted, "A lot of Wall Streeters are giving much thought to the subject of [home] building stocks in view of the current peace talk."

By October 1970, when the market had pulled out of its

decline, textbook publishers had been singled out as beneficiaries of the peace dividend. "The thinking goes that as the Vietnam war is scaled down, a bigger slice of the Federal budget will be allocated to education," noted the "Heard on the Street" column on October 2, 1970. The column quoted an analyst, " 'The war is the factor in determining different allocations for funds.' "

As the war dragged on, however, the peace dividend became smaller and smaller. The plight of the aerospace industry in 1970–71 proved that at least it was vulnerable to defense cutbacks, especially when the civilian market failed to take up the slack. Boomlets in various peace stocks didn't last. Peace news still moved the market, but skepticism set in much more quickly.

By the time serious peace negotiations actually began in the fall of 1972, articles about the expected effects of peace were much different from those of 1968. Stories about the defense industry no longer talked about beating swords into plowshares, but rather about how once the war was over more money could be spent on fancy new weapons systems, sophisticated military aircraft, and whatnot. "The Defense Department will have more money to spend on advanced state-of-the-art stuff when it doesn't have to buy helmets and boots," an official of General Dynamics Corp. told the *New York Times*.[6]

Indeed, the defense budget presented for fiscal 1973 was only $1.5 billion less than spending in fiscal 1968, a far cry from the $30 billion that government officials had been talking about. In July 1972, the Pentagon issued a report on defense spending in general and Vietnam in particular. Its explanation of what happened to the peace dividend in terms of the military budget is reproduced in Table 8-B. By the time the war actually ended there wasn't anything left over; stepped-up war operations in the last months added $3.7 billion to the cost of the war, Defense Department accountants said.

The peace-and-the-economy stories began featuring quotes like this one in the Chicago *Sun-Times* of October 29, 1972.

[Robert Genetski, an economist at the Harris Bank & Trust Co.] puts it this way: "We don't think the end of the bombing and of mili-

Table 8-B.   The Evaporating Peace Dividend

	($ Billions)
Military budget spending in FY 1968 was	78.0
Military and civil service manpower cut 1,440,000 (30%) and purchases from industry cut (in real terms) by 40%—these cuts should have reduced spending by	−24.0
So FY 1973 spending, at FY 1968 pay rates and price levels, would be	54.0
But we must add pay raises for personnel remaining, plus increased costs of military retirement	16.3
Purchase inflation (22%)	6.2
So FY 1973 spending is	76.5

Source: "The Economics of Defense Spending; A Look at the Realities," Department of Defense (Comptroller), July 1972, p. 150.

tary operations will have any great impact on the economy either way. People have tended to overestimate the amount of the spending that would be cut out and the number of people that would be released [from military service]. . . .

The real effect of peace would be mainly psychological, many of these stories said. Chicago *Sun-Times* financial columnist Edwin Darby wrote, "Down the road it may move a businessman to decide that he can okay the plans for a factory or give the plant foreman the extra help he's been wanting. The young couple may pick the 19-foot refrigerator with the ice maker instead of the 15-foot without."[7]

The market bounded upward in the fall of 1972, and many analysts credited the seeming progress toward peace, along with good economic news. "The explanation for the market's spurt seems to be this: The war has been a poison to the body politic, a cloud on the business outlook. It has been like a low-grade fever, sapping the enthusiasm of consumers and businessmen," wrote Peter S. Nagan of the Newhouse News Service.[8] Of course, it didn't hurt that the peace negotiations between Henry Kissinger and Le Duc Tho were surrounded by the utmost secrecy so that investors would grasp at every rumor, buy when the two negotiators left a session smiling, and practically lose themselves in ecstasy over a remark such as "Peace is at hand." *Barron's* Alan Abelson noted, "Long quiet stretches of uncertainty, broken only by thunderclaps of unexpected news, are not exactly conducive to tranquility on Wall Street, where the emotional norm is a shade either side of hysteria."[9]

Peace Arrives

At 10:49 A.M., Eastern Standard Time, on Tuesday, January 23, 1973, the Dow Jones' News Service tapped out an item from Paris that Henry Kissinger and Le Duc Tho apparently had initialed a Vietnam peace agreement. It was confirmed that evening when President Nixon announced a "peace with honor."

On Wednesday, January 24, the Dow Jones Industrial Average declined more than 14 points—the sharpest daily drop in seventeen months. Earlier that day, the market staged its final peace rally by gaining 4 points. "There wasn't any question of a rally on a cease-fire agreement," observed one broker. "It was just a question of how long; this one lasted only an hour."

Many brokers and investors were surprised by the decline and said it was merely profit-taking. But it was more than that, and the signs had become evident the previous week when strong rumors of peace—including bald hints in President Nixon's inaugural address—made little difference to the market. Investors ceased speculating on the benefits of peace when they were confronted again with a fresh wave of inflation, the consequences of which by this time were much more predictable.

Earlier in January, President Nixon had lifted the mandatory wage-price restraints of Phase 2 and replaced them with a voluntary system called Phase 3. At first, the business and financial communities cheered this move, but then they had second thoughts about the ability of Phase 3 to keep inflation in check. Similar doubts were entertained overseas, where currency speculators began drubbing the dollar again, which eventually led to the second devaluation in little more than a year.

By the time the Vietnam peace finally arrived, investors were watching another act in the center ring—fast-rising interest rates and galloping consumer prices. As one broker put it, "In the framework of Phase 3, the peace issue lost its bounce." Thus did Vietnam cease its direct influence on the market, though it still cast a shadow through its legacy of economic dislocations.

Summary and Conclusions

The Vietnam experience doesn't completely answer the question of whether war is good for the market, but it does prompt some observations. For one thing, there was strong market enthusiasm for peace in the final years of the war, a phenomenon that was missing during the Korean conflict. Either investors had changed their minds about war in general, or they had come to regard its economic consequences more seriously. The Hanson-Russett study, cited earlier, offered this analysis.

> Perhaps by the 1960s investors had begun to decide that inflation may boost stock prices, but at the same time it may decrease corporate profits and dividend values. Tax increases and the introduction of controls to curb inflation tend to have—at least in the short run—a further negative impact on profits. . . . Such a changed attitude toward inflation could be part of an increasing appreciation among investors of the destabilizing effects of war upon the economy and the difficulty of selecting, timing, and legislating the appropriate combination of measures that would make a war economy substantially more profitable than a peacetime one.[10]

If that's so, it suggests the market's reaction to the prospect of war is more complex than simply positive or negative. A small brushfire conflict might stimulate military spending and be good for business, but once the little war goes past a certain limit it might cause undesirable side effects that negate the earlier gains. An investor with this viewpoint would be expected to be bullish on escalation when the war was small, but bearish on escalation and bullish on de-escalation when the war became large, which is exactly how the market acted regarding Vietnam.

There are unanswered questions, however. Market responses might be very different to a war begun in a period of recession rather than in prosperity, as were both Vietnam and Korea. Also, investors may distinguish between war and defense spending; war is economically risky, but a sustained high level of defense spending may be both attractive and conducive to the type of economic planning needed to avoid painful, drastic adjustments.

Notes

1. Philip A. Fisher, *Common Stocks and Uncommon Profits,* (Harper, 1960) 2nd ed., pp. 128–129.
2. Albert R. Karr, "Business & Vietnam," *Wall Street Journal,* February 4, 1966, p. 1.
3. Betty C. Hanson and Bruce M. Russett, "Testing Some Economic Interpretations of American Intervention: Korea, Indochina, and the Stock Market," in *Studies in International Relations and Foreign Policy,* ed. Steven Rosen (D. C. Heath, 1973), p. 233.
4. Victor J. Hillery, "Dovish Wall Street," *Wall Street Journal,* March 6, 1968, p. 1.
5. "Planning for Peace," *Wall Street Journal,* June 19, 1968, p. 1.
6. Philip Shabecoff, "Defense Industry Adapting to Peace," *New York Times,* December 3, 1972, Section 3, p. 1.
7. Edwin Darby, "Peace in Vietnam and the Economy," Chicago *Sun-Times,* October 29, 1972, p. 98.
8. Peter S. Nagan, "What Peace Will Bring," Newhouse News Service, Chicago *Daily News,* October 4, 1972, p. 41.
9. Alan Abelson, "Up and Down Wall Street," *Barron's,* January 22, 1973, p. 1.
10. Hanson and Russett, "Testing Some Economic Interpretations," pp. 242–243.

9

Presidential Elections and the Market

I⊤ was early summer 1972, and the setting was a private room in an exclusive midwestern businessmen's club. The officers of a small but rapidly growing company were meeting with the top men of a brokerage and underwriting firm to map details of a common stock offering that would take the company into the public realm several months hence. Drinks and lunch were being digested, and the president of the company that was going public admitted that something was troubling him.

"This election coming up—how do you think it will affect the market when our shares come out?" he asked.

The syndication man for the brokerage firm leaned back in his chair and smiled. "If you tell me who's going to win and what he'll do once he gets elected, I might give you an answer," he said. "Otherwise, I haven't the faintest idea."

The answer was notable for its diffidence, because over the years Wall Street has accumulated quite a bit of lore about how the stock market behaves before, during, and after presidential elections, and many of its inhabitants will offer an opinion with very little prompting. Out of it all, however, comes precious little on which to hang one's hat, or, more pointedly, one's portfolio.

Nevertheless, one thing about which there can be no doubt is that presidential politics dominates the news as do few other subjects. Attention is most intense during the months immediately preceding the quadrennial balloting, of course; during election years events of all sorts, including economic ones, are weighed primarily for their supposed impact on how the voters will decide on the first Tuesday in November.

There also is no real question about such attention being misplaced. The modern U.S. presidency is the world's most powerful position, and its holder's ability to shape events is unequaled. He can commit U.S. troops to foreign conflicts virtually on his own hook (President Truman did it in Korea in 1950; Presidents Kennedy, Johnson, and Nixon waged war in Vietnam with only the most general approval of Congress). The president is the prime mover behind the nation's vital taxing and spending policies. He can institute wage and price controls. He appoints the heads of the executive departments and the members of the federal commissions that closely regulate business. In all of those functions he can greatly influence the factors that go into the evaluation of common stocks.

The manner in which a president goes about his duties—the tone of his leadership—often has been interpreted as a market-affecting factor. A good many observers, for instance, laid the blame for the steep stock market decline of 1962 squarely on the doorstep of President Kennedy. They said that the business community "lacked confidence" in him as a result of a series of decisions that culminated in his angry denunciation of the steel companies that raised their prices in April of that year. His statement "My father always told me that all businessmen were sons-of-bitches, but I never believed it till now," which surfaced while he was doing battle with steel magnates, didn't help things much, either.*

Eliot Janeway, the financial commentator, fastens on still another aspect of presidential conduct as a key market determinant—his relationship with Congress. "When the president and the Congress work in harmony together, and when the **president** proposes and Congress disposes, *no* [italics ours] negative pressures to which the stock market is subjected can keep it down," he wrote. "Contrariwise, when a breach develops between the president and the Congress, when the president moves but doesn't lead, *no* [italics ours] expansive pressures which conventional analysis identifies as constructive can hold the stock market up."[1]

Using this yardstick, Mr. Janeway traces the post-World War I market crash to the conflict between President Wilson and Senator Lodge, the 1929 crash to what he calls "President Hoover's breach with Congress," the 1946 decline to President Truman's feud with Senator Taft, and so on.

One needn't, of course, subscribe to such theories to recognize the impact that presidential policies and demeanor can have on stocks. But the question remains whether it really matters to the stock market which of the two major political parties controls the White House, and whether the prospect of a victory of one over the other is enough in itself to influence its course.

The Long View

On the surface, it might be assumed that the market would fare best under a Republican president. The Republicans, after all, are widely regarded as the party of big business, and, in fact, most business leaders and other well-to-do types who account for the bulk of market activity are numbered in their ranks. Thus, it stands to reason that they would be better disposed toward investing in stocks when one of their own is running things.

A look at the market's past performance records shows that this hasn't been the case, however. In the 50 years from 1923

---

* Another widely repeated anecdote of the period went like this. Kennedy to businessman: "If I weren't president right now, I'd be buying stocks." Businessman to Kennedy: "If you weren't president, I'd be buying stocks, too."

through 1972, Democrats have been in the White House for 28 years and Republicans for 22. The stock market advanced in 19 of the Democratic years and declined in 9, while "plus" years outnumbered "minus" ones by just 12 to 10 under Republican presidents.

In light of this, one might expect the market to perform best during election years in which a Democratic victory seems imminent, but this hasn't been true, either. Democrats won 7 of the 13 presidential races during the 1923–72 period, but stocks showed net gains in only 4 of those election years (1936, 1944, 1960, and 1964). By contrast, the market rose in each of the 6 election years since 1923 in which Republicans emerged triumphant (1924, 1928, 1952, 1956, 1968, and 1972).

Well, then, if the mere prospect of a Republican victory is enough to buoy stocks, then the actual election of one should have the same effect, right? Wrong again. In 4 of the 5 years immediately after Republicans won election or reelection to the White House in the last 50 years, stocks dropped. In 5 of the 7 years that followed Democratic victories, they posted gains.

All this is pretty confusing, so another tack might be in order. *Newsweek*'s "Wall Street" columnist Clem Morgello searched the records back to 1900 and found that presidential election years generally have been good for the stock market. The Dow Jones Industrial Average, he reported, rose during 12 of the 18 election years between 1900 and 1968, and 1972s rise made it 13 of 19. He also discovered a big difference between election years in which the incumbent party was returned to office and years when it was turned out. In years when the ins stayed in, the DJIA rose at an annual average of 17.5%, but when they were bumped, it declined by an average of 5.7%.[2]

Postelection years long have been singled out as difficult ones for the market, no matter which party wins. Three of the worst declines in this century—in 1929, 1937, and 1969—all followed presidential balloting. Less severe slumps also occurred in the postelection years of 1941, 1949, 1953, and 1957, to name a few.

The common explanation for this good-year–bad-year

syndrome is that the party in power goes all out to keep the economy expanding (or, at least, make it appear to be expanding) in years that it must face the voters, but after the results are in, whoever takes charge often must do the painful things that were neglected while the electorate was being wooed.

This certainly contains some truth, but it overlooks some obvious and important considerations. Many of the postelection year declines also can be attributed to turns for the worse in the U.S. economy or the international situation. The Great Depression began in 1929. War in Europe haunted the market between 1937 and 1941 and is generally blamed for the steady stock price declines of that period. The years 1949, 1953, 1957, and 1969 were in part recession years.

A president beginning a new term might well feel he can risk economy-contracting policies in his first year in office, but it would seem that the seeds of any recession or foreign military conflict would lie elsewhere. It would be hard to argue that the mere fact that a year follows a presidential election would supersede these more basic considerations.

The observation that a falling market often signals a switch in party control of the White House might be a valuable guide to political pundits, but it is of doubtful use to investors.

In all, the history of stock market trends on or around election years provides some insight into investor mentality, but little else. More tangible clues to the market's long-range direction would seem to lie elsewhere.

The Short View

The previous discussion, however, should not be construed to mean that stocks do not react to political developments around election time; they do. As we have seen, the market upturn that began in March 1968 received much of its impetus from President Johnson's announcement that he would not seek reelection and that he would de-escalate the war in Vietnam. The rally that followed his statement was attributed more to the peace hopes it raised than to any overwhelming desire of investors to be rid of

Mr. Johnson, during whose tenure stocks fared quite well, but the political side of his statement can't be ignored.[3]

By the same token, the market upturn of late 1972, which sent a DJIA closing price over the 1,000 mark for the first time, was set off by the October 26 statement of Henry Kissinger, President Nixon's foreign policy adviser, that peace in Vietnam was "at hand" and the consequent assurance of a landslide victory for Mr. Nixon over Senator McGovern, who was highly unpopular with big business.

Those two incidents, though, were far more significant and dramatic than the usual election-year news fare. Traditionally, the news in the months leading up to the balloting has consisted mainly of the talk of the campaign—the speeches, charges, denials, and countercharges. This may be interesting enough, but political scientists tell us it has precious little effect on the electorate and, by implication, investors. Numerous studies have shown that the vast majority of the population decides who it will vote for as soon as the major party nominating conventions are over, and tunes out later arguments that might conflict with that choice.

But since the end of World War II a different sort of news event has entered the political equation—the national presidential preference poll. The pollsters made an inauspicious debut in the national eye by picking Dewey to defeat Truman in 1948, but they have since refined their sampling and interviewing techniques to the point where they can gauge the mood of the electorate to within one or two percent by talking to a relative handful of voters.

The preelection polls have come to play an important role in election coverage in the press. They show who is winning, and that is what elections are all about. Over a period of time, they indicate the comparative effectiveness of the candidates' appeals. Finally, they serve uniquely to introduce voters to the existence of opinions different from their own. Writes public opinion researcher Charles K. Atkin, "Polls [may overcome] selective exposure barriers, as voters of varying predispositions read opinion poll reports for their general interest value. Thus, many voters may become acquainted with information contrary to their present views, and the chance for conversion is greater than with the normal political content of the mass media." [4]

It would seem, then, that to measure the reaction of the stock market to the currents of election-year politics, we should turn to the polls as our barometer. This we have done for the last four presidential campaigns, each of which followed a distinctly different pattern—a narrow victory for a Democratic challenger (Kennedy in 1960), a landslide victory for a Democratic incumbent (Johnson in 1964), a narrow victory for a Republican challenger (Nixon in 1968), and a landslide victory for a Republican incumbent (Nixon in 1972).

Charts 9-1 through 9-4 show the weekly movements of the DJIA for the three months before and after election day in those four years. The charts for the years 1964 and 1972 (9-2 and 9-4) can be reviewed quickly, because in both those elections incumbent presidents held substantial leads in the widely circulated Gallup Poll (and other polls) from start to finish, and their victories were never seriously in doubt. Their challengers, the Republican Goldwater in 1964 and the Democrat McGovern in 1972, captured their nominations in fractious intraparty struggles that all but nullified their chances to win at the polls in November.

In 1964, President Johnson's lead over Senator Goldwater in the preelection Gallup Polls ranged from 28% to 36% with between 6% and 10% of those polled undecided. Goldwater won over most of the undecideds, but Johnson's margin in the actual voting was a wide 61.3% to 38.7%. An approving stock market moved upward from the beginning of August through the third week of November, tailed off for three weeks, and then resumed an upward path that was to continue into 1966.

President Nixon's lead over Senator McGovern in the 1972 Gallup Polls began at 19% (56% to 37% with 7% undecided) and increased steadily thereafter. His margin after the votes were counted was virtually the same as Johnson's eight years before.

The market dallied around the 950 mark until the week before the voting and then shot up swiftly, buoyed by the Nixon

Chart 9-1. Election Year-1960

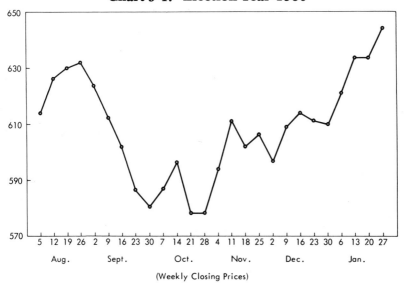

(Weekly Closing Prices)

Chart 9-2. Election Year-1964

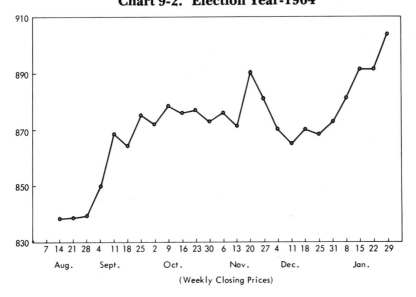

(Weekly Closing Prices)

Chart 9-3. Election Year-1968

(Weekly Closing Prices)

Chart 9-4. Election Year-1972

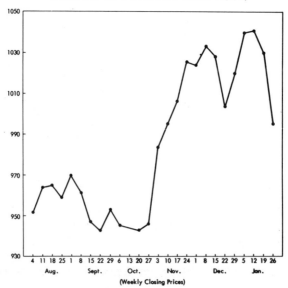

(Weekly Closing Prices)

victory and the apparent imminence of peace in Vietnam. It turned downward in January after the Watergate scandal and a plethora of other national problems began to reassert themselves.

The elections of 1960 and 1968 were much closer and thus merit closer attention. The campaign of 1960 was unusual in that the candidate that started off ahead in the polls wound up losing. The Gallup Polls during the preelection period are shown in Table 9-A. By election eve the candidates were in a virtual tie and

Table 9-A. Gallup Polls before the Election of 1960

Publication Date	Kennedy	Nixon	Undecided
Aug. 17	44%	50%	6%
Aug. 31	47	47	6
Sept. 14	48	47	5
Oct. 12	49	46	5
Oct. 25	49	45	6
Nov. 6	49	48	3

the Gallup organization called the outcome too close to predict. Mr. Kennedy's final margin of victory in the popular vote was a thin 50.1% to 49.9%.

From August through October, the pattern of the DJIA mirrored the fortunes of candidate Nixon, as investors seemed to follow their Republican inclinations. It climbed through August while the better-known vice-president led in the polls and dropped in September as Senator Kennedy, campaigning strongly, forged into the lead.

Stocks hit a low point in the last week of September, the week of the first and most important of the televised "great debates" between the candidates. Political analysts gave an edge to Mr. Kennedy in that crucial confrontation, and the polls showed that the voters agreed. Mr. Kennedy achieved his widest Gallup Poll lead in the survey released October 25, and the market sagged in response.

In the final week of the campaign, President Eisenhower took to the stump in support of his vice-president, and Mr. Nixon narrowed the gap. The market rallied.

But then the votes were counted, Mr. Kennedy won, and the market advanced again. It continued to climb throughout 1961. As in 1964, there was no postelection slump that year.

The pattern of the campaign of 1968 was quite different from that of 1960. Mr. Nixon again was the Republican nominee, but he went into the contest with a far more substantial lead in the polls than he had in his first try at the office. The Democrats were in disarray. President Johnson had stepped aside earlier in the year and the Chicago nominating convention that picked Vice-President Hubert Humphrey to succeed him was marked by violent antiwar riots in the streets of that city. Television brought the tumult into the homes of millions of Americans, and the impression it left did not bode well for the Democrats' retention of their eight-year hold on the White House.

Moreover, there was a third candidate in the field—Governor George Wallace of Alabama—who had made his mark in national politics as a symbol of southern resistance to racial desegregation. He was showing potent appeal among the northern blue-collar voters who had long been a bulwark of the Democrats.

The first Gallup Poll reading of the campaign, issued on September 14, gave Mr. Nixon 43% of the vote, Mr. Humphrey 31%, and Mr. Wallace 19%, with 7% listed as undecided. Those figures varied by only one or two percent in Gallup's next two samplings, which were released on September 28 and October 9.

As Chart 9-3 shows, the stock market was decidedly bullish from early August until mid-October, the period in which a Republican victory seemed assured. Even the turmoil of August's Democratic National Convention didn't cause stocks to pause; indeed, the market accelerated through that ordeal.

The sole break in the preelection upturn coincided with the period in which it became apparent that Mr. Humphrey's strength was on the rise. The final three Gallup Polls of the campaign, reflecting that surge, are shown in Table 9-B.

Table 9-B.   The Final Three Gallup Polls before the Election of 1968

Publication Date	Nixon	Humphrey	Wallace	Undecided
Oct. 21	43%	31%	20%	6%
Oct. 26	44	36	15	5
Nov. 3	42	40	14	4

As in 1960, the pollster's last tally was so close that it precluded a prediction of the winner. The DJIA on Monday, November 4, the day before the voting, stood at 946, down 21 points from its October 21 preelection peak of 967.

Mr. Nixon skinned through, however; his final margin over Mr. Humphrey in the popular vote was a bare 43.4% to 43%, with Mr. Wallace getting 13.6%. The DJIA moved up strongly for four straight weeks after the votes were counted. It turned downward for a time around the first of the new year, and then embarked on an irregular upward path that was to last until mid-May, when the bear market of 1969 took hold.

Summary and Conclusions

A look at the course of the DJIA in the months just *before* the last four presidential elections shows that the market did best in 1968 and 1972, the years when a Republican victory seemed likely. This seems to verify investors' rooting interest in the candidates of that party.

But in all four of the election years, no matter which party won or by how much, the DJIA closed in November higher than it had opened the month. Furthermore, in each of the postelection years save one— 1973—stocks showed early-year strength.

These latter patterns might be attributable to the release of the tensions and uncertainties that build up during any presidential election, even ones in which the outcome seems preordained. More probably, though, it reflects the recurrent conclusion of investor-voters of all persuasions that the guy who won might not be so bad after all. The stock market, at least in the short run, seems to give a newly elected president the benefit of the doubt until economic news forces a different view.

Notes

1. Eliot Janeway, "Politics and the Stock Market," in *The Anatomy of Wall Street*, ed. Charles J. Rolo and George J. Nelson (Lippincott, 1968), pp. 204–205.
2. Clem Morgello, "Wall Street: In an Election Year," *Newsweek*, July 10, 1972, p. 75.
3. "Stocks and Politics," *Wall Street Journal*, April 2, 1968, p. 1.
4. Charles K. Atkin, "The Impact of Political Poll Reports on Candidates and Issue Preference," *Journalism Quarterly*, Autumn, 1969, p. 515.

10

Cleaning Up: Pollution and Stocks

Nᴀᴛɪᴏɴᴀʟ elections in the United States have the satisfying quality of being regular; we've had one every fourth November, no matter what else was happening. In the interim, though, investors must cope with a constantly changing batch of social issues that bob in and out of the news in a seemingly unpredictable way. As a nation, we have long embraced the notion that we have a sacred duty to make things continually better for everybody, and thus we are easily stirred to action by revelations that we are less than perfect in some respect. Such revelations, no matter how frequent, always seem to come as something of a surprise, which ensures their place as a staple of the news media.

Whether an issue makes a splash in the stock market is by no means certain, however; some of the biggest have caused nary a ripple. The black civil rights movement, for instance, has been an important factor in the news since the mid-1950s, but there has been no evidence of a "civil rights market" or "black equality stocks."

But some social issues do have pronounced stock market

implications. The Soviet surprise launching of Sputnik in 1957 not only accelerated the U.S. space program, mightily benefiting aerospace contractors, but it also precipitated an almost panicky effort to improve public education, especially in science. This boosted the stocks of textbook publishers and makers of educational products. Likewise, concern about the availability of health care for the elderly led to the passage of Medicare legislation, which in turn propelled the stocks of hospital supply firms, nursing homes, and drug manufacturers. Similarly, the sexual revolution and worry about population growth gave impetus to birth control stocks.

But the social issue with perhaps the greatest impact on stocks in the late 1960s and early 1970s was the concern about the quality of the physical environment. The environmental movement challenged traditional cultural values and long-standing industrial practices. It had a strong impact on stocks because it was self-evidently a money issue. Companies and governmental units were being pressed to shell out to clean up, and someone was bound to profit.

The pollution issue, we think, provides a handy vehicle for exploring how a social concern can be translated into stock market action. It's a timely one, too, because at this writing the economic implications of the cleanup movement have yet to be fully realized. Like other issues, it didn't spring upon the public full-blown. Its development followed the same general pattern that has been taken by many other topics that have gained the national stage in recent years. In broad outline, the process seems to go like this:

Early Stage—A few dedicated crusaders attempt to stir up the issue, occasionally generating some publicity but scoring few accomplishments; there is no measurable impact on the stock market.

Second Stage—More and more people become involved in the issue, and leaders on both sides tend to take extreme stands. If the issue is one that affects stocks, market action is likely to be volatile. News coverage of the issue and its effects becomes intense.

Third Stage—Emotionalism lessens, and the extreme positions taken earlier are moderated. This is reflected in news coverage that takes on a less excited, more temperate tone. Market action continues, but stocks lose some of their volatility.

Final Stage—The issue is absorbed into everyday life and thus ceases to be an issue. Market action may or may not continue, depending on the nature of the issue, but if it does it will be responsive to the influences that affect stocks generally and not to developments pertaining to the issue itself.

These stages can't be applied dogmatically. It isn't always possible to see where one step ends and the next begins, nor do issues necessarily proceed smoothly from step to step; witness the apparent stagnation of the black civil rights movement in the early 1970s. On the other hand, the sequence at least provides a helpful context in which to view the endless parade of issues and how they might influence the stock market.

It also might be noted that modern social issues are to an increasing extent creatures of the mass media. Newspapers, magazines, and TV may not create these issues, but they are instrumental in elevating them to positions of national concern. The fact that nearly everybody is now reached by the media has accelerated the development of issues, we believe. Thus, close attention to the news is more necessary than ever in spotting emerging issues early enough to make investment decisions based on them pay off.

A Broad Background

Concern for the environment didn't arrive in the 1970s unannounced. In the United States, water pollution had become a recognized problem by 1899, when Congress passed the Refuse Act, still in force today, to regulate the dumping of wastes. Air pollution had been an irritant at least since the dawn of the industrial revolution.

But pollution became a lot worse in the years after World War II as both industry and the population mushroomed. Pioneer environmentalists laid the blame in two directions, as described in a *Business Week* commentary.

The Sierra Club, Environmental Action, and other groups charged that a "technological determinism" had taken hold: If we were capable of doing something, we did it, without due regard to the social consequences. Like Mt. Everest, the technological heights were scaled just because they were there.

The second argument, advanced by environmentalist [Barry] Commoner, held that industry, in pursuit of higher profits and productivity, had displaced older technologies with more environmentally damaging products and processes. Thus, phosphate detergents displaced soap, one-way bottles and cans outsold returnables, gasoline-gulping cars muscled out economy vehicles, non-degradable plastics replaced paper packaging, synthetic fibers won markets from cotton and wool, and energy-intensive aluminum production took over from steel and lumber. These technological shifts, Commoner said, were more important than either population or economic growth in bringing on the environmental crisis.

Though Commoner's analysis was at least partly true, he failed to see that the crisis was also due to our failure to use the technology we already had. To this day, one-third of all Americans (including the residents of Manhattan) have no primary sewage treatment—even though the technology has been available for decades. Similarly, some utilities have not installed stack controls—even though precipitators were invented nearly 50 years ago. Furthermore, though some control technology is presently unavailable... effective regulation could spur its development.[1]

The environmental movement got rolling in the early 1960s, helped by publicity generated by such things as the best-selling book *Silent Spring*, by Rachel Carson. The environmentalists were not naive idealists. They geared their pitch in large part to politicians and succeeded in getting several bills passed that added momentum to the movement. Table 10-A shows the key federal legislation that helped institutionalize the environmental issue in the U.S. economy. Note that the legislative pace began accelerating considerably in the late 1960s and early 1970s.

Another indication of how rapidly the environmental movement caught fire is the number of technical publications on pollution and pollution control. These are now put out by the U.S. Environmental Protection Agency, which lists them all in a 73-page

Table 10-A.   Major Pollution Control Legislation

1899	Refuse Act
1948	Federal Water Pollution Control Act
1955	Air Pollution Act
1956	Water Pollution Control Act Amendments
1957	Air Quality Act
1963	Clean Air Act
1965	Solid Waste Disposal Act
1965	Motor Vehicle Pollution Control Act
1965	Water Quality Act
1966	Clean Waters Restoration Act
1967	Air Quality Act
1969	National Environmental Protection Act
1970	Water Quality Improvement Act
1970	Resource Recovery Act
1970	Clean Air Act
1970	Noise Pollution and Abatement Act
1972	Water Pollution Control Act Amendments
1972	Federal Environmental Pesticide Control Act
1972	Noise Control Act

bibliography. Table 10-B shows the number of these publications by the year they were issued. The same snowballing effect is apparent as it was with the legislation, although it peaks a year or so

Table 10-B.   Number of Technical Publications on Pollution and Pollution Control by Year

1960—1	1967—27
1962—1	1968—55
1963—5	1969—121
1964—6	1970—226
1965—15	1971—346
1966—13	1972—160

later because most of the studies were dependent on the legislation for funding.

The legislation and technical publications were important for another reason. They formed the basis of much of the media coverage of the environmental issue and thus were instrumental in shaping the national attitude. The technical studies traced the extent of pollution down to the local level, and the news stories about them gave the lay public a close-to-home view of the issue and prompted their demands for fast action. The many stories about the legislation, as each bill moved toward approval, seemed to indicate that action was indeed being taken and high-powered action, at that. Pollution control bills called for sizable appropriations, and in their debates, the politicians spoke of needing to spend billions of dollars for pollution control.

Wall Street bit hard.

An "Industry" Emerges

The way the environmental issue had been presented led investors to an inescapable conclusion. If pollution was as bad as it was said to be, and if the government was going to spend, and make industry spend, a lot of money to clean things up, then who was going to do the cleaning up? Why, the pollution control "industry," of course.

Except that there was no such industry. What there was were diverse companies making air and water purification devices, which investors and analysts hastily agglomerated into an "industry." In reality, noted Argus Research Corp., a stock market research firm, in an analysis in late 1970, "the field of environmental pollution control is comprised of a wide variety of different businesses. Some have existed for decades, others are just beginning to emerge. For the most part, these various businesses have little relationship to each other in terms of manufacturing methods, marketing and demand factors. That each plays some role in controlling or avoiding environmental pollution is, of course, a type of common denominator. This does not mean, however, that every segment of the field will experience similar rates of growth or that investors will find affluence by indiscriminately plunging into every company that claims a role in controlling effluence."

Nevertheless, investor demand decreed that there be an industry, and so there was one. Sniffing the excitement over this new group of companies, some brokers began touting the stocks as surefire money-makers. One of them told the *Wall Street Journal*, "Everyone is concerned about the problem—government, business and the public. And a lot of dough is being spent to get rid of air and water pollutants. Stocks in these companies have no where to go but up."[2]

Indeed they did. As an example, take Research-Cottrell, a company that had been making air purification equipment since 1912, and which went public in May 1967. The offering price of the shares was $14, and from there the price advanced more than a point a minute in the first 20 minutes of trading. Four months later, when the stock was listed on the American Stock Exchange, the price was around $50. A year after the company went public the stock was selling as high as $150. It closed at a peak of $165.62½ in August 1968 before splitting three-for-one.

Standard & Poor's Corp. began keeping track of pollution control stocks as early as 1965, and in that year the price-earnings ratio of the group was 30% below that of the S&P Industrials. By 1968 the pollution group's P/E ratio was double the industrials' and by 1969 it was almost triple.

Not surprisingly, such market play attracted a lot of companies to the pollution control industry. In the first edition of the Pollution Control Directory, published in 1968–69 by the American Chemical Society, 650 companies listed some 6,000 types of products. In the 1972–73 edition, 2,000 companies listed 15,000 kinds of products.

Most of the companies entering the field were legitimate, but some other newcomers, warned a *Wall Street Journal* story,

...are questionable ventures apparently set up to capitalize on what's becoming a hot stock-market trend. Besides a rash of new concerns with bewilderingly similar names based on the words environment, ecology and pollution, some older companies with only slim ties to the field are being promoted as pollution-control concerns.

"I've seen companies call themselves air pollution-control companies because they make things like furnace filters," complains James G. Wilcock, president of Joy Manufacturing Co., a major producer of equipment to reduce air pollution.[3]

One company that decided to take a ride on the pollution bandwagon was a little outfit based in Miami called Southern Gulf Utilities, which was in the water and sewage treatment business. Early in 1968, it announced it was entering the air pollution control and waste disposal fields, and it changed its name to Ecological Science Corp. By late summer rumors were circulating that this was to be the really big winner in pollution control, and the company's stock zoomed to $66.50 from its 1967 close of $24.

As it turned out, Ecological Science was more public relations form than pollution control substance. From December 1967 to December 1969, the Securities and Exchange Commission later charged, the company issued 90 news releases, "many of which didn't report substantial events but which served only to create an image of activity in pollution control." The company doctored its financial reports, put out inaccurate information about its products, and touted itself relentlessly to analysts.[4]

The troubled company was sued by shareholders and creditors and placed in the hands of a limited receiver. The SEC suspended trading in the stock from May 1971 to mid-December 1972; it reopened over-the-counter at about $1 a share. The image-promoting management was forced out in 1972 and a new board of directors attempted to put Ecological Science back on its feet.

Other new companies debuted much less flamboyantly and still commanded a premium in the stock market. For instance, Envirotech Corp. was formed in May 1969 by combining a subsidiary of Ogden Corp., a conglomerate that processed food and made various kinds of equipment, and a subsidiary of Bangor Punta Corp., a diversified maker of recreational and industrial products. At that time, Ogden had a P/E ratio of 15 and Bangor Punta's multiple was 13. When Envirotech went public in 1971, its offering price of $32.50 was 29 times its fiscal 1971 earnings. By the close of 1972, Envirotech's P/E ratio had climbed to 37, while Ogden was selling at 8 times earnings and Bangor Punta at 16 times.

Similarly, in 1972 Trans Union Corp. spun off its pollution control subsidiary, Ecodyne Corp. By early 1973, Ecodyne was selling for 32 times earnings, while Trans Union, which retained 85% ownership in Ecodyne, was selling for a multiple of only 16.

Market Performance

How pollution stocks did in relation to the rest of the market is shown in Chart 10-1. The movement of the market as a whole clearly regulated the swings in pollution stocks most of the time, except that the pollution group was much more volatile in the early years. From late 1966 to early 1967, for example, the market advanced 25% but the pollution group, in its first flush of investor recognition, doubled.

There were a couple of exceptions worth noting. One of them

Chart 10-1. Market Performance of Pollution Control Stocks

Source: Standard & Poor's Corp.

occurred in late 1969 and early 1970, when the pollution group shook off the general bear market for a while and staged a rally. This countertrend was in large part a release of optimism that had been built up by news of pending legislation and other factors, such as President Nixon's 1970 State of the Union message in which he called for "a new quality of life in America and restoration of nature to its natural state."

"The buying is all psychological," said Roland Williams, a pollution control specialist for E. F. Hutton & Co., in the *Journal's* "Heard on the Street" column of January 7, 1970. "Based on fundamentals . . . there isn't any doubt but that people have let their enthusiasm run away with them. But it could run further, even though most price-earnings multiples are outlandishly high." He cited "recent heavy publicity" as a major cause of the enthusiasm.

"Anything the government says about pollution really moves the group," said Dorothy Fels, head of research for Parker-Hunter Inc., Pittsburgh. Virginia Davisson of Harris Upham & Co., New York, observed, "The price action of [pollution control] stocks mirrors what has seemingly become a yearly pattern: remarkable strength in the first part of each year. Whether or not it is happenstance, the performance appears to anticipate the President's annual environmental message to Congress and the political one-up-manship that invariably follows."

Another exception occurred in 1972, when the pollution group peaked in the first four months and declined thereafter despite the market's strength late in the year. Vietnam peace hopes hadn't failed to boost pollution stocks before. One reason for this uncharacteristic downturn was described in "Heard on the Street," September 9.

> Let an industry leader talk negatively about his business. And then pity the poor investor with holdings in that field.
>
> It happened about a month ago when Research-Cottrell (American), considered by many the premier company in the pollution control field, talked about a slowdown in new orders. The result: Its stock has tumbled about 20%, although it still sells at about 55 times

earnings. And the stocks of many other companies in the pollution control field with high price-earnings multiples also dropped. . . . Blaming the slowdown on such problems as standardization and delays in governmental approval of new projects, [Research-Cottrell president John E.] Schork says "the business is out there and eventually it will come."

But the multibillion-dollar spending estimates that did so much to buoy the pollution stocks in earlier years were no longer carrying so much weight on Wall Street.

When the environmental issue first began to emerge, estimates were that $50 billion to $75 billion would be needed for adequate pollution control. By 1970, the highest private estimates had reached $85 billion—$95 billion for just the next five years, and in 1971, the Environmental Protection Agency itself put a price tag of $105.2 billion on the cost of five-year compliance. In 1972, the EPA said $287 billion would be spent on pollution controls in the ten years through 1980. These were the figures that had helped attract eager investors to the pollution control stocks. But how much of that would be spent for the actual hardware that the pollution control companies were selling? Only 10% to 15% at the most, and in some instances as little as 3%, according to the top analysts of the field. The bulk of the money would be spent on construction, labor, nonglamorous items such as cement and pipe, and operating expenses, they said.

Of course, even though the real market was much smaller than what had been indicated, it still was growing rapidly. But the big numbers had attracted so many companies to the field that the smaller-than-expected pie was being sliced into more and more pieces. Donald DeVries, a vice president of Koppers Co., which makes some air pollution equipment, told the *Wall Street Journal;* "The profits are overrated (in pollution control equipment). Everyone thinks this is the greatest thing since 'the pill' and that they ought to get in on it. (As a result,) everytime you turn around there's someone new (in competition with you)."[5]

Late in 1969, Joy Mfg., which long had been in air pollution control equipment, announced it was "examining" a major move into water pollution control. Six months later Joy said it would enter the water field only in a very limited way. "We looked into it very carefully, and we weren't terribly impressed with the profits they were making in that field," recalled Andre Horn, financial vice president.

Leading analysts had been harping on these negative factors in 1971 and 1972, but it took a while for investors to catch on. "You can tell people and tell people to stay away, but they still jumped in and bought this junk, and many of them got hurt," remarked Mrs. Davisson of Harris-Upham.

One reason for the lag in the impact of negative information was that pollution control stocks were, at least in the beginning, the darlings of the public and not institutional investors, who tend to be very sensitive to negative news and react in unison. Edmund Lee, a pollution control analyst, told a round table discussion in early 1971 about the difficulty of interesting most institutional investors in his field.

> Every time I went to a fund to talk about pollution, I spent most of my time explaining basics. They have very little knowledge of what's going on. . . . By the time you educate them, the play is already gone for that particular swing and they don't want any part of it.[6]

There were other reasons for the lack of institutional interest, of course. Many of the attractive pollution control companies had very small floats, so big mutual funds and other institutions couldn't acquire enough shares to make a worthwhile holding.

But what it all amounted to was that the boom in pollution control stocks was much more the product of individual public investors than institutions. The public was caught up in the environmental issue, so the bad news of smaller sales, elusive profits, and occasional flimflam took awhile to sink in. When it did, investors who once had bought on the wildest estimates began to look harder at present and future profits and at the P/E ratios they were being asked to pay for them.

The Issue Matures

Another important factor in the cooling enthusiasm for pollution control stocks was that by 1972 the environmental issue itself had mellowed. That's not to say that people had lost interest in it—to the contrary. In the 1972 elections taxpayers across the country approved bond issues relating to pollution control projects but turned down hundreds of others. The emotional fervor, however, that had brought out thousands of people on the first Earth Day in 1970 had diminished.

This in itself was not surprising; nothing can generate a high pitch of commitment and interest among a broad, diverse segment of the population indefinitely. Another moderating factor was the realization that pollution cleanup would take years and meanwhile people still had to work and live. Economist Milton Friedman expressed this point of view in a February 1973 interview in *Playboy* magazine.

> Even the most ardent environmentalist doesn't really want to stop pollution. If he thinks about it . . . he wants to have the *right amount* of pollution. We can't really *afford* to eliminate it—not without abandoning all the benefits of technology that we not only enjoy but on which we depend. So the answer is to allow only pollution that's worth what it costs, and not any pollution that isn't worth what it costs. . . . It's a fact of life that there are hard, nasty problems that can be mitigated but not eliminated. This is one of them.[7]

Another moderating influence in 1972 was the growing awareness of an impending energy crisis. Experts warned that the United States was using more energy of all sorts than it was producing and that shortages would occur, which they did in various places in 1973. Many factors contributed to the energy crisis, but the environmental issue clearly was one of them. Environmental considerations had stalled construction of a pipeline to bring oil from Alaska, had delayed construction and operation of several nuclear electric generating plants, had sharply cut the use of coal, and so on. It became increasingly evident that environmental priorities would have to be reconsidered if the United States productive machinery was to keep growing.

One of the first important examples of this occurred in April 1973, when the EPA reluctantly gave the auto makers a year's extension to meet exhaust-emission standards originally required for

1976-model cars. The EPA cited "potential societal disruption" as a reason for the extension.

And so, the issue mellowed. The effect in the market was to reinforce the changing attitudes that were evolving independently from closer examination of the pollution control industry— namely, less propensity toward euphoria and a greater tendency to evaluate pollution control stocks by more concrete and conventional criteria.

The Negative Influence

In addition to the positive influence on pollution control stocks, the environmental issue had a negative influence on the stocks of companies and industries that were doing the polluting and would have to pay billions of dollars to clean up. Of necessity, our broad-brush approach becomes even broader at this point because it is impossible to quantify a negative influence in the market. There isn't any way of measuring what wasn't or what might have been.

Table 10-C indicates which industries were most affected by the environmental issue and how they increased their expenditures to comply with pollution regulations. Generally, the industries showing the biggest gains in pollution control spending were the ones most negatively influenced in the market.

The impact showed up in a number of important ways. One of them was earnings. Higher pollution control expenditures typically meant lower profits for many companies, which in turn resulted in a lower stock price. For some companies it was the rate of profitability rather than actual dollar profits that declined. In any event, the effect was the same.

Price-earnings ratios sometimes also reflected the negative influence of the environmental issue. Consider this analysis of General Motors by David Healy of Burnham & Co. in October 1972.

> Until not too long ago, the stock market believed that General Motors' dominant industry position, wide profit margins, strong finances and liberal dividend policy should merit a P-E ratio of 13–14 times normal earnings. Now that the company, as the world's largest

Table 10-C. **The Importance of Pollution Abatement in Capital Spending for Selected Industries**

	1970	1971	1972*	1973*
	(Percent of Capital Expenditures)			
Iron and Steel	7.1	9.0	13.9	14.5
Non-Ferrous Metals	7.4	10.3	23.6	20.1
Electrical Machinery	1.0	2.2	3.1	3.6
Non-Electrical Machinery	2.1	5.0	4.1	5.9
Motor Vehicles & Parts†	5.1	5.5	6.3	9.4
Aerospace†	2.7	5.0	6.5	2.3
Stone, Clay, Glass	13.4	22.9	18.1	23.1
Other Durable Goods	6.2	11.3	15.0	14.9
Food and Beverage	2.5	3.9	⋅5.0	4.9
Textile Mill Products	2.8	4.6	4.8	4.0
Paper & Allied Products	6.1	17.4	29.1	25.6
Chemicals & Allied Products	5.4	8.4	8.9	10.0
Rubber Products†	3.5	4.0	5.0	5.2
Mining	3.6	3.0	9.3	11.3

*Projected. †Small sample.

Source: Lionel D. Edie & Co. *1973 Capital Expenditure Intentions of Private Industry*, April 1973.

and most profitable business enterprise, is beset by environmentalists, union leaders, social reformers, government regulations, crusading senators, minority groups and class-action plaintiffs, the market grudgingly allows General Motors a P-E ratio of ten. The key question does not seem to be whether General Motors' earnings and dividends will rise; that seems relatively assured as the public appetite for new cars continues to improve as economic conditions strengthen. The question is whether General Motors will continue to be regulated, sued, laundered, struck, and threatened with breakup to the extent that the downward revaluation of the P-E ratio will become permanent or worsen. Although the question probably is more in the realm of sociology than investment analysis, our answer is a qualified "yes," and we have been stressing other auto stocks for purchase [except where yield is a factor] despite the General Motors stock's statistical cheapness by historical standards.

Other analysts also cited pollution control problems in their security recommendations. For instance, Robert A. Hageman of Argus Research wrote on January 27, 1972, that because of the problems Phelps Dodge was having in complying with tough Arizona air pollution regulations, "both speculative and investment accounts should switch into other more attractive vehicles."

The Securities and Exchange Commission was anxious that pollution problems not come as a surprise to investors. In 1973, the SEC adopted amendments to several of its forms that require disclosure in stock registrations and various other reports of any "material" effect on capital expenditures, earnings, and the competitive position of the company and its subsidiaries that resulted from compliance with environmental laws.

Summary and Conclusions

Not all social issues affect the stock market, but those that do can exert tremendous influence. Many issues seem to follow a similar pattern of evolution—they emerge slowly, blaze intensely for a while and then are resolved in one fashion or another. This pattern is reflected in stock market action—if any—that is connected with the issue.

In some cases, though, issues leave a permanent footprint on the market. In the case of the pollution issue, it seems probable that the pollution control "industry" will survive as a separate entity. This would keep the subject in the financial news even after the issue itself had faded from the front pages. If so, pollution control stocks would be judged by normal investment criteria and not by the emotionalism and excitement surrounding the social issue.

Another task to which a basically qualitative approach to the evaluation of news can be put is in determining how the stocks of individual companies responded to the news that involved them. This we do in the next three chapters. We view some news items differently by relating them to individual stock movements rather than to the market as a whole. Stock splits, management changes, and the like have little influence on the general market, but they certainly do affect specific issues. So far, we have been looking at stocks through a news telescope; now, we switch to a microscope.

Notes

1. "Technology Isn't the Villain—After All," *Business Week*, February 3, 1973, p. 38.
2. Dan Dorfman, "Heard on the Street," *Wall Street Journal*, September 23, 1968, p. 33.
3. James P. Gannon, "Cleaning Up," *Wall Street Journal*, February 13, 1970, p. 1.
4. "Ecological Science Corp. Accused by SEC On Promotional Drive, Consents to Order," *Wall Street Journal*, May 3, 1971, p. 6.
5. Gannon, "Cleaning Up," p. 1.
6. "Pollution Control, A Roundtable Discussion," *The Wall Street Transcript*, reprint, March 1971, p. 16.
7. "Playboy Interview: Milton Friedman," *Playboy*, February 1973, pp. 58–59.

Part IV

Company Profiles

11

Curtiss-Wright: A Cork on the Waves

"There are some stocks that are almost impossible to analyze on either a fundamental or technical basis," Eastman-Dillon, Union Securities & Co. informed its customers in a March 1972 market research letter.

These issues usually are referred to as "concept stocks." An examination of some of the concept stocks of the past reveals certain factors which are common.

1. *Simplicity*—The appeal of each stock was based on an easily grasped idea, which indicated that significant sales and earnings growth seemed almost inevitable.

2. *Exclusivity*—The easily grasped idea was unique to the particular company involved.

3. *Performance*—The stock performed extremely well in the market place and subsequently began to feed on its own success.

4. *Elusiveness*—The potential market or earnings to be derived by the company was not possible to quantify.

This brief essay was in preface to an Eastman-Dillon report on

Curtiss-Wright Corp., which was emerging as one of the hottest contenders to become the IBM or Xerox of the 1970s. The concept that fueled Curtiss-Wright's shares on the New York Stock Exchange was the Wankel rotary engine, which had been developed by German inventor Felix Wankel in 1954 and on which Curtiss-Wright, through a combination of foresight and luck, had secured exclusive North American rights in 1958.

While the workings of the Wankel were well known to only a handful of engineers in 1972, and its operating qualities still were very much a matter of debate, its economic implications for Curtiss-Wright certainly met the test of simplicity—the company would be rolling in royalty money if the Wankel supplanted the piston engine as the prime power plant in American-made cars. The company's exclusive right to license American Wankel manufacturing, which it obtained for just $2.1 million, satisfied the second criterion.

Performance? The stock was selling for $28 a share when the report was issued, up from $11 just three months before. It was to climb as high as $59 a share before sliding back to the 30s at year-end (see Chart 11-1).

And the stock clearly met the test of elusiveness. Although giant General Motors Corp. had previously contracted with Curtiss-Wright to adapt the engine for its own use on a flat-fee basis, in early 1972 no one had the foggiest notion how many cars, or boats, or airplanes, or lawnmowers, or whatnot would be built around the Wankel, and when. Moreover, Curtiss-Wright's tight-lipped silence about its licensing negotiations with other potential producers precluded solid estimates of what the company would receive if the Wankel did catch on.

But to Eastman-Dillon's four criteria for a "concept stock" we would add a fifth—extreme susceptibility to good and bad news in its crucial early stage of development. This feature, we think, stems from the difficulty of pinning down what the future holds for the company behind the stock. If facts are lacking, opinion will suffice. If anything is possible, one "expert's" opinion is as good as the next's, providing it obtains comparable circulation.

Chart 11-1. Curtiss-Wright Weekly Movements-1972
(Closing Prices)

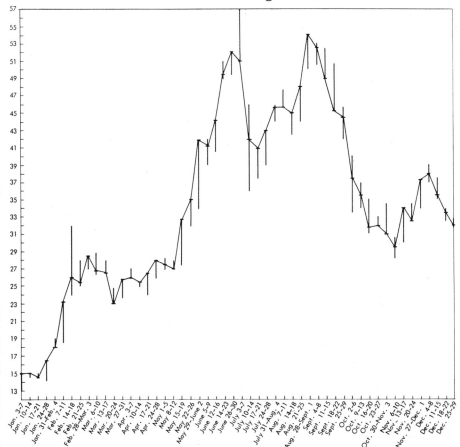

The budding concept stock is a cork on the waves of the news, and a good many facts must accumulate before the sea becomes calmer and clearer. In the meantime, riches await the person who can spot a new Wall Street concept in its infancy and correctly evaluate the deluge of information that accompanies its ascent.

The Company

As the 1970s began, few companies seemed less likely candidates for Wall Street stardom than Curtiss-Wright. The company, based in Wood-Ridge, New Jersey, had an illustrious enough past. It was formed in 1929 through a merger of the Wright Corp., founded by aviation pioneers Orville and Wilbur Wright, and Curtiss Aeroplane and Motor Corp., whose founder was Glenn H. Curtiss, another key figure in the early days of flight. The company made an important contribution to aviation in the 1930s, and its efforts during World War II were monumental. Between 1941 and 1945, it turned out 26,000 airplanes, 143,000 aircraft engines, and 146,000 electric propellers, emerging from the conflict as one of the nation's largest industrial concerns.

From there on, however, Curtiss-Wright's record was less impressive. In the late 1940s, when aviation was changing from propeller power to jets, the company neglected to put up the research money to participate in the new field and lost its largest single market to United Aircraft Corp.'s Pratt-Whitney Division.

For the next 20 years, Curtiss-Wright wandered in and out of a number of industrial fields, ranging from nuclear components to sand and gravel excavation. Some of the ventures were profitable and some weren't. The company was caught seriously short again in the cutback of U.S. aerospace and military spending in the late 1960s and was forced to withdraw from a number of areas. Losses from discontinued operations figured prominently in a net loss of $4.6 million in 1970, compared to a profit of $12.3 million, or $1.36 a share, the previous year. Sales in both years totaled about $280 million.

The company turned into the black again in 1971, but only slightly; there were more write-offs, and earnings equaled just 18 cents a share. Some problems continued: It lost money on the manufacture of nuclear components because it underestimated the costly nature of the highly precise work.

This spotty record cast Curtiss-Wright into disrepute on Wall Street for much of the postwar period, and the style of its management added to its woes. The company's chief executive from 1949 to 1960 was the flamboyant Roy T. Hurley, whose forecasts of company prospects often fell well short of being realized. Mr. Hurley's successor, T. Roland Berner, was a lawyer who was considerably more restrained in his public pronouncements, but little more loved by the investment community. The company was consistently but unspectacularly profitable during the growth-conscious 1960s, and the stock remained rooted between $10 and $20 a share for almost the entire decade.

The Wankel Engine

One thing that Curtiss-Wright did right during the Hurley era was acquire rights to the Wankel, but in characteristic fashion it managed to turn even that into a liability at first. In November 1959, about a year after the company made the purchase, Mr. Hurley called a New York press conference to proclaim that Curtiss-Wright had made the engine work and was set to put it into production the next year. The Wankel had fewer moving parts than the conventional piston engine and could deliver twice the power while taking up half as much space, he said, adding that it would be priced competitively with existing engines.

When the Wankel was put into independent hands, however, it quickly became apparent that it wasn't nearly ready to be manufactured. Its durability was nil, it consumed gasoline in vast quantities, it was costly to make, and it was considered dirty even at a time before air pollution had become a national concern. Many ticketed it for the same junk heap that held the numerous other "revolutionary" new engines that had surfaced over the years. Curtiss-Wright's credibility, none too strong to begin with, suffered another blow.

But rather than pull out, Curtiss-Wright and another license holder, Audi-NSU of West Germany, a subsidiary of Volkswagen, set out to correct the engine's flaws. In the next ten years, Curtiss-

Wright alone spent more than $25 million on engine refinements, securing more than 100 patents in the process. In 1961, Toyo Kogyo Ltd., a small Japanese automaker, acquired a license to make the engine for its own use and launched a parallel development program.

The rotary engine that stirred the stock market in 1972 operated on the same principles as the one Felix Wankel first designed. Instead of the up-and-down motion of the pistons in the conventional engine, the Wankel employed a triangular rotor that spun around inside a spherical combustion chamber. An air-gas mixture entered through a port, was compressed as the rotor turned, and was ignited by a spark plug. The rotor then swept out the waste products through another port as the cycle continued.

The up-down piston action of the conventional engine had to be converted into torque by connecting rods and cranks; the spinning rotor turned the main shaft of a vehicle directly. For this and other reasons, the Wankel needed fewer moving parts, which meant that theoretically there was less to go wrong. Its more efficient design produced more horsepower from a smaller and lighter unit, giving auto designers some welcome leeway.

The main problems with the early Wankels centered on the seals that lined the curved edges and apexes of the rotor—they tended to break down quickly under the heat and pressure of use. By 1970, however, both Curtiss-Wright and Toyo Kogyo claimed to have found suitable materials for the seals, and they assertedly had solved other problems, including fuel consumption. Toyo Kogyo began exporting its rotary-powered Mazda autos to the United States in 1971, and the model received good reviews for its quick acceleration and vibration-free ride.

More than that, however, was required to make the Wankel a hot item in 1972. Even if the engine lived up to its supporters' most glowing claims, it would cost automakers and other users billions of dollars to retool to produce it on a large scale, and such expenditures wouldn't be taken lightly. Moreover, the rotary wasn't the only new engine bidding to capture Detroit's favor. Chrysler Corp. had invested heavily in developing a gas turbine engine. Steam and battery-powered cars had their advocates. And a considerable amount of work was underway to make the beloved piston engine a more suitable instrument for future use.

But two other potent factors pushed the Wankel to the forefront. One was the tight new federal pollution controls that were to take effect in 1975 and 1976. Despite all of its refinements the Wankel still was considered a "dirty" engine in 1972 (how dirty was a subject of controversy), but its small size seemed to give it a crucial edge in this regard because it allowed more room under the hood for the emission control devices that would be needed to meet the tough standards.

The second was the mounting speculation that General Motors was about to start equipping at least some of its cars with Wankels. This in itself would not greatly benefit Curtiss-Wright. General Motors' contract with the company and other prime license holders called for payments of $50 million over six years, and nothing more. If GM didn't terminate the pact, which it could do unilaterally at the end of any year before 1975, Curtiss-Wright would receive a total of $22.7 million. The rest was to be split between Audi-NSU and Lonrho Ltd. of England, which had purchased Dr. Wankel's rights.

All other potential producers of Wankels were being asked to pay continuing royalties to those three companies, with the proceeds to be divided as shown in Table 11-A. It was from these

Table 11-A. **Distribution of Wankel Engine Royalty Payments among License Holders***

	Engines Produced in N. America	Engines Produced Outside N. America	Engines Produced Outside N. America but Imported into U.S.
Curtiss-Wright	60%	10%	75%
Audi-NSU	24	54	15
Lonrho Ltd.	16	36	10

*Source: W. E. Hutton & Co.

payments that the speculation over Curtiss-Wright's future income centered.

General Motors received special treatment because it was the largest of the U.S. automakers, and other manufacturers would be obliged to follow wherever it led in the important matter of a new engine. If General Motors adopted the Wankel wholeheartedly, Curtiss-Wright's fortune was made.

Oppenheimer & Co., a brokerage house with a large institutional following, said in a research report dated September 25, 1972, that if the Wankel achieved 100% penetration of the U.S. auto market by 1980, the royalty payments to Curtiss-Wright from this source alone at $5 an engine would add $4.82 to the company's per-share earnings; if the payments were reinvested to yield an after-tax return of 10%, the figure would climb to $6.04 a share. By 1989, Wankel royalties alone could boost the company's earnings by as much as $6.33 a share, and that figure would soar to $21.65 a share if the royalties were invested to yield 10%, Oppenheimer said.

The Questions

Thus, Curtiss-Wright entered 1972 with dazzling prospects and also with several large questions remaining to be answered in the news columns.

The first and foremost question concerned the plans of General Motors. The company could drop the engine at any time, proceed full-steam ahead, or do something in between. Every whisper about GM's intentions sent brokers' phones ringing until the corporation finally revealed its plans.

The second question concerned the plans of Ford and Chrysler, the second- and third-ranking producers. Curtiss-Wright would stop receiving income from General Motors in 1975, no matter how many Wankel-equipped cars GM built, so further income depended on its concluding royalty agreements with Ford and Chrysler, and, less importantly, makers of other conveyances and motor-driven machines.

Third was the performance of the engine itself. Not everyone agreed that the Wankel was all Curtiss-Wright and its other advocates said it was. The engine could drive the little Mazda, but what about larger cars? What about durability? What about fuel economy?

Fourth, what were the terms of the royalty agreements that Curtiss-Wright was trying to negotiate with engine makers and how strong was the company's basic right to license manufacture of the engine in the United States, Canada, and Mexico? The former point was in doubt because Curtiss-Wright wouldn't discuss it. The latter stemmed from persistent rumors that it might be possible to end-run the company and make the engine without cutting it in.

The final question might best be stated this way: What were the stock market "experts" saying? This factor is important to the performance of any stock, but it applies especially to volatile, highly speculative issues such as Curtiss-Wright. The budding "concept stock" trades in an atmosphere of hopes and dreams. It feeds on opinions that support exalted expectations and is vulnerable to contrary expressions, no matter what their basis.

The Prelude

For a stock that was to respond sharply to any breath of news during its period of maximum activity, Curtiss-Wright penetrated the public consciousness rather slowly. As we have seen, the Wankel engine wasn't unknown as the 1970s began, but it wasn't taken seriously by any save its most enthusiastic boosters. Even the announcement of General Motors' 1970 agreement to develop the engine didn't much pique Wall Street's interest; automakers were looking at several new engine possibilities at the time, there was no special hurry in finding one, and $50 million wasn't all that much for a company of GM's size to spend.

What started the ball rolling were two articles that appeared in the press just days apart in early October 1971. The thrusts of the stories were different but their theme was the same—the Wankel worked.

The front page of the *Wall Street Journal* of October 1 carried the news that the Wankel-powered Mazda had become the talk of car-conscious California, where it had just been introduced. Some 85,000 persons jammed Mazda showrooms in the first few days the model went on sale, the largest crowds to show up for a new car debut since right after World War II, the paper reported. And how did the car run? It had a pickup "like a scalded cat," the *Journal's* reporter said.

The *Wall Street Journal* story didn't mention Curtiss-Wright, but some people made the connection because the company's stock jumped to $12.25 a share from $11 that day.

The second article probably had the greater impact because it was more detailed, prominently featured Curtiss-Wright's role in Wankel development and raised the vital pollution issue. It ran in the *New York Times Sunday Magazine* of October 3. Its author was George Alexander, science editor of *Newsweek*. We will quote from it extensively because it was widely reprinted and contained many of the elements that were to fuel the subsequent boom of Curtiss-Wright's stock.

The article's opening paragraph gave a clear indication of its tone. "The hottest thing on wheels these days is also on boats, snowmobiles, power tools and factory floors. It is the Wankel rotary engine—an internal combustion machine of unusual design that is more compact, lighter and mechanically far simpler than a reciprocating piston motor of equivalent horsepower. These are precisely the sort of advantages that make engineers stand up and take notice, and, judging from the increasing number of firms around the world that are taking out licenses to manufacture this German invention, it seems safe to predict that there's a Wankel in your future."*

It continued, "There has been considerable speculation that General Motors will introduce a small, two-seat commuter automobile—powered by a Wankel—by the mid-1970s. [Note: It didn't.] There have also been rumors that GM is considering the Wankel for some of its existing model lines."

The article then launched into an explanation, illustrated by drawings, of how the Wankel worked, why its emissions could be

* © 1971/1972 by The New York Times Company. Reprinted by permission.

controlled more easily than those of the piston engine, and what work Curtiss-Wright had done to perfect the engine's troublesome seals. The author test-drove a Wankel-powered car and liked it for its lack of vibration and ease of handling at all speeds.

What were the Wankel's prospects as an auto power plant? For this, the author turned to David Cole, a University of Michigan engineering professor who had headed a team that tested the engine's pollution characteristics and came away a booster. Professor Cole's words carried particular weight because his father, Edward Cole, was president of General Motors. "I'd say there's a 75% chance that by 1980 the predominant American auto engine will be the Wankel," he said.

And what of Edward Cole? Estimates that the Wankel would be powering GM cars by 1976 were "conservative," he was quoted as saying, with a grin.

In the two days following the publication of the article, Curtiss-Wright stock jumped another $1 a share to $13.25. Then reaction set in—Wall Street had touted the Wankel before—and the stock slipped back to the $10–$11 level by mid-November.

Late in the year, however, the Wankel got another boost when *Reader's Digest,* whose circulation of almost 18 million made it by far the nation's most widely read general interest periodical, reprinted the Alexander piece in its January issue, which came on the newsstands the week of December 27. Curtiss-Wright stock rose from $12.25 a share to $13.50 in the five trading days preceding year-end.

Usually, word about a hot new stock emanates outwardly from the brokerage houses, but this time the process was reversed, at least initially. "We started getting calls from customers who had read about the Wankel and wanted to know what it was all about," said a customers' man at one large Wall Street firm. "We asked our research boys, and they didn't know too much about it. They looked into it, and liked what they saw."

Interest picked up considerably with the new year. Several brokerage firms hired engineers to come in and brief their analysts and salesmen on the Wankel. On January 6, the New York Society of Security Analysts assembled a panel of experts to explain the engine's workings at an open meeting. The session was well attended. According to several persons who were there, the analysts came away impressed.

Curtiss-Wright presented Wall Street with something of a problem, however. Brokerage houses—at least the larger ones—do not relish going on record recommending highly speculative issues —and Curtiss-Wright was just that—for fear of being blamed if things turn sour. The company could scarcely rate a "buy" on the basis of its earnings performance or the record of its management. Moreover, the company wouldn't discuss its Wankel outlook or much else, leaving estimates solely to the analysts. That was too long a limb for most firms to go out on. So while numerous houses reported on the engine and the company during the year, most made no trading recommendations, or at least advised only the brave to buy.

A few written reports on the Wankel were circulating on Wall Street in early 1972, the most comprehensive of which was published by W. E. Hutton & Co. Curtiss-Wright rated only brief mention in it; several automotive machine tool suppliers were singled out as the most likely investment prospects.

The Rise

The word on the engine was out, though, and if brokerage houses shield away from publicly recommending Curtiss-Wright, many of their salesmen didn't hesitate to do so privately. "A lot of phone calls were placed," said one broker who followed the stock closely.

On January 27, three weeks after the New York analysts met, the stock made its first great upward surge. From a January 26 close of $14.75 it went to $19 on January 31, making the most-active list on a 2½-point gain that day. There was a week's pause and then the run-up resumed. On February 9, Curtiss-Wright gained 2⅜ points to close at $22.375. On February 15 it rose 2⅞ to $26.75. The next day it was up $5.25 a share to $32, topping the most-active list with 467,000 shares traded.

The business press took only passing notice of the stock's movement through early February. On February 10, the *Wall Street Journal* carried a brief item in "Abreast of the Market," quoting a Curtiss-Wright official as being unable to account for the previous day's rise. However, the activity of February 15 and 16 spurred the newspaper into action.

"An excess dosage of speculative fever is the reaction of several Wall Street analysts to the sharp run-up in Curtiss-Wright shares," the *Journal's* Dan Dorfman wrote in his "Heard on the Street" column of February 17. "Sources believe that part of the excess speculation is attributable to the mistaken notion that General Motors' right to build Wankel rotary engines involves royalties to Wankel rights holders. Not so. . . . It's understood that GM is ready to start making a limited number of Wankel engines using its own technology. But this isn't a sign it is getting into commercial production. . . . Further, there aren't any negotiations involving Curtiss-Wright with any other U.S. automaker."

Curtiss-Wright stock reacted to the item, closing February 17 at $31, down $1 on the enormous volume of 979,000 shares, almost 12% of its 8.3 million common shares outstanding.

The next day, Dorfman again focused on the Wankel boom, quoting Edward J. Giblin, president of Ex-Cell-O, a machine toolmaker. "Based on what I know about the Wankel engine, the speculative fever [in Curtiss-Wright and the machine tool stocks] is overdone. We see nothing indicating there will be any release of orders for machine tools for the Wankel engine. And I don't think there's any assurance that the Wankel engine will be the engine of the future."

Curtiss-Wright dropped almost five points to $26.125 upon release of the story, again leading the most-active list on volume of 562,000 shares, lifting its volume for the week to about 2.5 million shares. Much of the activity consisted of in-and-out trading by brokerage firms for their own accounts, it was understood.

The two *Journal* items put a damper on the Curtiss-Wright boom. Between the February 18 sell-off and mid-May, the stock hovered between $23 and $28 a share, well below its February 16 high. Throughout those three months, however, news about the company and the Wankel kept accumulating, and most of it was good. The steady stream of favorable reports not only kept the stock from sliding back to its level of the previous year, but also prepared the way for the next major run-up.

On February 28, Richard C. Gerstenberg, General Motors' chairman, announced that his company was making "good progress" in solving the technical problems of the Wankel, but cautioned that "our work hasn't progressed to the point to warrant any production commitments for rotary-powered cars at this time." The *Journal* called the statement "qualified and cautious," but it sent Curtiss-Wright stock up almost 3 points to $28.50 that day, reversing a brief slide.

Consumer Reports featured the Mazda in its April 1972 issue, which went on the newsstands March 20. The car had its faults, the magazine said—gas mileage was worse than that of other imported subcompacts, oil consumption was relatively high, and it "bucked" when lightly accelerated on low-speed turns—but it got good reviews overall. "Toyo Kogyo seems . . . to have overcome the bugs that have restrained the Wankel engine's progress," the magazine reported.

On March 27, Curtiss-Wright announced that it earned $1.5 million, or 18 cents a share, in 1971, against the loss of the year before. The company also commented favorably, though vaguely, on prospects for the Wankel, saying "its superiority over existing engines should dramatically increase as it finds its way into more applications." The statement sparked a two-day advance of the stock of $2.75 to $25.75, stemming a two-week downturn.

Two technical journals got into the act the next month. *Popular Science* featured the Wankel on the cover of its May issue, which came out April 27. The article inside predicted, though incorrectly, that GM would begin producing Wankel-powered cars in October 1973, and predicted that "in ten years, the Wankel revolution should be complete." The story was worth two points to Curtiss-Wright stock the day it appeared.

Ward's Auto World addressed a May article to Curtiss-

Wright's stake in the Wankel, giving featured attention to the company's right to authorize American production. "If you go with the Wankel, will Curtiss-Wright get a piece of the action?" the magazine asked John J. Riccardo, Chrysler's president. His answer: "If we're going with the Wankel, we've got to deal with Curtiss-Wright. There's no other way. After all, they own the patents."

Curtiss-Wright held its annual meeting on May 7 in Wilmington, Delaware, and took the opportunity to declare that its Wankel was "cleaner" than the piston engine, even in the untreated state. "Those who say it is a dirty engine are wrong," said Chairman and President Berner. "The Curtiss-Wright rotary engine is better than any other rotary engine in the world."

All this set the stage for run-up number two, which began on May 18. The trigger this time was the anticipation of what General Motors might announce at its annual meeting to be held the next day, a fact that was widely reported in the press. As it turned out, no definitive statement was forthcoming. Edward Cole repeated for the umpteenth time that the company hadn't made any firm production plans and that it *wouldn't* put the engine in 1974 models. However, a tantalizing tidbit did emerge from the session. "General Motors Corp. is nearing a key decision point in its Wankel engine development program," the *Wall Street Journal* reported. "GM's top management and directors are expected to look at the entire program next month, GM sources said. If they approve of what they see, the giant auto maker could move considerably closer to producing rotary engine cars within a few years."

Anything still was possible, and for the next three weeks the stock rose steadily, closing on Friday, June 9, at $41.25 a share.

The stock got another upward jolt from the news the following week. On June 13, Brunswick Corp. signed an agreement with Curtiss-Wright to make and market the Wankel for use in marine power plants. Brunswick was to pay Curtiss-Wright an initial fee plus a percentage royalty on engines produced. No other terms were revealed. It was the first sizable licensing pact Curtiss-Wright had landed in 1972. The news was carried on the business wires and that day the stock rose $5.25 a share to $45.875 on heavy trading.

The *Wall Street Journal* again took note of the Wankel boom on June 15 with a front-page story titled "Wondrous Wankel," which detailed the surge in the price of various stocks that had some connection with the engine, however tenuous. Its dominant theme was one of caution. "I think the market for rotary engines is very promising, but I think the stocks have run up too far and too fast on expectations of profits that are still very nebulous," Joseph Ronning, an analyst for Paine, Webber, Jackson and Curtis, was quoted as saying.

The story cost Curtiss-Wright a one-day loss of 3⅜ points, but the stock gained that all back and more by the month's end, closing on June 30 at $52 a share. Early the following week, *Fortune* came on the stands with a lengthy feature extolling the Mazda and predicting a bright future for the Wankel generally. The stock closed on July 5 at $57, its high closing price of the year.

Early the next day, a Thursday, the stock rose two more points before Reuters' news wire carried an item quoting Alan G. Loofbourrow, Chrysler's vice-president for engineering, as saying that the Wankel engines his company was testing were unimpressive; they used a lot of fuel, they backfired, and there were problems with the spark plugs. This time it was an auto executive who was knocking the Wankel (even if his firm had never been enthusiastic about it), and the stock fell out of bed, plunging more than eight points by the day's end. Trading on the stock was halted until late the following day, but when it opened no rally occurred.

On Saturday, the *New York Times'* Robert Metz devoted his "Market Place" column to Curtiss-Wright's stock market odyssey. The article mainly recapitulated the stock's price movements of the previous week, but called Curtiss-Wright a "curiously out-of-touch" concern and used the term "pie in the sky" in connection with the Wankel's prospects. On Monday, the stock lost another 5⅛ points.

On Tuesday, another blow: Reuters quoted a General Motors submission to the U.S. Environmental Protection Agency saying that its Wankels couldn't meet 1975 emissions standards without as much emission-control hardware as conventional engines. No one had ever claimed that the Wankel could meet the standards without the additional gear, but no matter. Trading on Curtiss-Wright stock was halted that day, and the next day it plunged nearly ten points to $36.125 a share.

By this time, Curtiss-Wright stock was reacting immediately to everything. On July 13, the Chicago *Tribune* carried a story saying that it had learned that General Motors had approved the production and sale of Wankel-powered cars for the fall of 1973. GM denied the story later in the day, but it also was disclosed that during the previous month company management had briefed directors extensively on the engine, and the session "went a long way toward winning them over to the project," the *Wall Street Journal* reported. Those two stories turned the tide and Curtiss-Wright stock moved back up by 5⅝ points.

The turnaround was to last more than a month. The stock gyrated around $42 a share until July 28, the day after Curtiss-Wright signed a license agreement permitting Ingersoll-Rand Co. to use the Wankel in its compressor, pump, and electric generator assemblies. The stock rose $3.75 on the news.

On August 17, the *Journal*'s front-page "Business Bulletin" column moved the stock up $2.375 in two days with an item saying that Ford was "quietly and energetically" pursuing its work on the Wankel even though the official corporate stance on the engine was "cool." The stock had lost several points during that week after the *New York Times* reported that Ford was taking another look at the Stirling engine, an external-combustion affair that had been rejected by carmakers 35 years before as being too heavy and complicated. Little more was heard about the Stirling after that.

Finally, on August 28, General Motors dropped the other shoe. In a four-paragraph statement, the company said it expected to start selling Wankel-powered, 1975-model Vegas late in 1974. No numbers were given, but industry sources predicted an initial run of 30,000 cars. It was the first official confirmation that GM was near production on the Wankel and it was thus historic because the Vegas would be the first cars GM ever made without piston engines. It also made it clear that the automaker would continue payments under its $50 million agreement with Curtiss-Wright and the other license holders through 1975.

The statement was tentative in some ways. It said that "engine development and manufacturing processing work would continue" on the engine, and that production would proceed *if* the work "progresses as anticipated." Yet it drove Curtiss-Wright's stock from $46.875 a share on August 28 to $54.75 at the close of trading on Friday, August 31.

The Fall

After that, however, it was mostly downhill for Curtiss-Wright. The reversal began slowly—a point here and a point there—but the trend soon was unmistakable. The drop no doubt stemmed partly from a broader stock market decline that was underway in September, but it was helped along by the news about the Wankel, which turned sour.

On September 3, Ford officials held a news conference in Detroit on various automotive subjects. Touching on the Wankel, Chairman Henry Ford II said that his company was working on various types of new engines but didn't expect to make any revolutionary changes in that area soon. President Lee Iacocca agreed that the Wankel still needed more work, and pointed out that Ford wouldn't commit itself "too quickly" to any expensive engine retooling. The statements cost Curtiss-Wright stock two points in as many days, sending it below $50.

On September 19, England's prestigious *Financial Times* carried the disquieting news that Audi-NSU had "quietly" shelved plans to put the engine in more of its cars soon. According to the newspaper, the simplest explanation for the move was that the Audi was selling well enough as it was, but it added that the company had experienced repair problems with some of the Wankel-powered RO 80 models it already was selling. Said the *Financial Times*, "The one thing that is certain about the Wankel engine is that it will not bring immediate wealth for sharp-eyed investors.

At best the rotary engine will be introduced gradually and slowly as an optional extra, at extra price, in standard cars. If these sell well it will be tried in other cars. If they do not, it will be withdrawn."

The same day, *Newsweek*'s "Wall Street" column appeared with much the same conclusions. "Brokers agreed" that the run-up in Wankel stocks had been based on a "pyramid of suppositions," wrote Clem Morgello. "They agree further that no one will make any really big money from the engine for three to five years and many of the stock recommendations employ earnings projections for 1980, which is a long time to wait for dinner."

Curtiss-Wright opened at $50.50 on September 19. By September 25 it was at $42.

The stock took its sharpest one-day drubbing of the slide—six points to $34.125—on October 4, the day the *Journal*'s Dan Dorfman devoted another column to it. The column said that "at least a couple of analysts" thought that the New York Stock Exchange had "abrogated its responsibility to the investing public" by not insisting that Curtiss-Wright reveal more about its Wankel negotiations. George Ulrich, author of the influential W. E. Hutton report on the engine, was quoted as saying he wasn't a strong believer in Curtiss-Wright because of its "poor record and a management that is far from aggressive." An unnamed analyst said that the company's price-earnings multiple anticipates that "everyone will not only drive a Wankel but eat them as well."

The stock slipped below $30 a share in early November on news that General Motors was holding talks with Japan's Honda Motor Co. on an engine that Honda had developed to meet the 1975 federal pollution standards.

Curtiss-Wright's shares rallied along with the rest of the market after the November election, topping $39 a share on December 7, but that was as high as it was to go. On December 9, a *Business Week* article titled "Detroit's Frantic Hunt for a Cleaner Engine" was subtitled "The Wankel is only one answer. Steam turbine, pistons and even batteries have a chance." Curtiss-Wright stock slipped again, closing the year at $32.

Even stories that might have buoyed the stock during its advance failed to save it from its late-year decline. On November 20, the Chicago *Tribune* ran another "exclusive" story saying that General Motors had stepped up its Wankel engine delivery plans because of design "breakthroughs." The stock slipped two more points that week.

Summary and Conclusions

Curtiss-Wright's stock caught on solely because the company had the Wankel engine, which in early 1972 looked like an idea whose time had come. The concept gained the public eye because of the attention it received in the press. Ordinary corporate news, such as sales and earnings reports, were virtually ignored by investors as a basis on which to buy or sell the stock.

Almost four months elapsed between the earliest important stories about the Wankel—in the *Wall Street Journal* and *New York Times Sunday Magazine*—and the stock's initial run-up. Once the stock began to move, it responded far more quickly to news, often on the day the stories hit the business news wire services.

By and large, the stories that moved the stock didn't relate to actual events involving the Wankel but rather to what various observers *thought* about the engine and its chances for success. Their opinions qualified as news because the Wankel stocks, particularly Curtiss-Wright, were news.

As long as Curtiss-Wright's return from its Wankel rights remained nebulous, the stock could weather adverse comment: witness its recovery from the *Wall Street Journal* columns of February 17 and 19 that dubbed speculation in the stock excessive, and its rebound from its four-day drop of 21 points triggered by the Chrysler executive's negative appraisal of the engine.

What stilled the Curtiss-Wright boom was a massive injection of fact, started by General Motors' August 28 announcement of its Wankel production plans. At first this seemed like good news, but it wasn't long before forecasts based on 100% Wankel use in autos by 1980 began to look farfetched in light of GM's modest first intentions. Subsequent stories about Ford's cautious stance on the engine and Audi-NSU's shelving of its Wankel plans lent further credence to the belief that no prospect of a Wankel revolution was at hand and that any changeover to the engine would be gradual.

It shouldn't be forgotten that despite its late-year decline, Curtiss-Wright's stock closed in 1972 at more than twice the level it entered the year. As such, it did not immediately qualify as a concept stock that failed. It is perhaps better to think of it as one that didn't succeed as quickly as many had hoped.

12

General Mills: Grandma Becomes Cinderella

ELEMENTS of novelty or glamor aren't necessary for a stock to become a Wall Street favorite. Exhibit A is General Mills Inc. As 1971 ended, the company was about as familiar as any on the national scene. Every child, past and present, knew about it. It was the company that made Wheaties, the Breakfast of Champions, and Cheerios, those crunchy little circles of oaty goodness. In the old days, the company sponsored the radio adventures of the Lone Ranger, every boy's hero. Heroes were harder to come by in the more cynical seventies, but the company was still in there pitching its breakfast cereals to the kids on the Saturday morning television cartoon shows.

Every housewife knew about General Mills. It was the company that made those handy cake and pancake mixes under the imprimatur of Betty Crocker, the all-American homemaker. There never was a *real* Betty Crocker; she was invented by General Mills' marketing men in the 1920s and updated periodically to give the gals at home someone to identify with—a kind of Lone

Ranger of domesticity. No matter, though—the deception was a small one and the products sold well.

Everyone on Wall Street knew about General Mills, too, but from the middle 1960s until the early 1970s the associations there were less than fond. Breakfast was going out of style in the frantic and fragmented families of middle-class America, and the company's attempts to diversify out of this bind were slow in paying off. In the five fiscal years of 1967 through 1971, General Mills' per-share profits crept upward at the un-Wheaties-like annual rate of 5.4%, and the company's stock went nowhere on the New York Stock Exchange. Except for a brief foray above $40 a share in the 1968 bull market and a plunge to the low twenties in the downturn of 1970, the stock lingered between $25 and $35 a share for the entire period from 1965 to late 1971. Wall Street dubbed it a "GNP stock": solid and reliable enough, but dull.

Wittingly or not, this also was the image that emanated from General Mills' steel-and-glass headquarters in Golden Valley, Minnesota, a suburb of Minneapolis. Beginning in late 1967, the company's chief executive was James P. McFarland, a small, alert man who reached the top after an arduous climb through the corporation's ranks of 33 years, ten of which were spent as a salesman and sales manager in a company outpost in Great Falls, Montana.

Jim McFarland made it to the top by dint of ability, to be sure, but he had other qualities that endeared him to the senior officers and directors of General Mills. These included unswerving corporate devotion (he once told the *Wall Street Journal* that he quit smoking cigarettes during his Montana days because he felt they hindered his sales performance), personal modesty, and a reputation as an "operations man" dedicated to producing profits through the manufacture and sale of products rather than by the more spectacular means of acquiring other concerns.

Louis F. ("Bo") Polk, who had been considered Mr. McFarland's chief rival for the General Mills' presidency, was quite another sort. Young, lanky, and colloquial, he entered the company as a computer expert, financial planner, and acquisitions man, quickly attaining a vice-presidency and a national reputation as a business whiz kid. His aim was to make General Mills a kind of "growth company" that constantly acquires new businesses and spins off old ones.

When it came down to the final choice, though, Jim McFarland won hands down. Explained Charles Bell, son of the company's founder and its chairman when Mr. McFarland ascended to the presidency: "We felt that Jim's stability was something that was best for the company. We believed that he'd keep things in balance. He wasn't the wheeling, dealing type who might go off on a wild tangent."[1]

In brief, neither General Mills nor Jim McFarland, who moved to the chairmanship in 1969, seemed likely to capture the fancy of the concept-conscious men of Wall Street, but that's exactly what happened. The company's stock moved out of its rut in late November 1971, climbing from $34 to $41.50 by year-end. It continued to rise steadily to a high of $63.75 on December 29, the final trading day of 1972. Its 1972 gain of 55% almost quadrupled the 14.6% rise in the Dow Jones Industrial Average, making it one of the year's biggest winners on the Big Board.

The kind of news that heralded General Mills' 1971–72 stock price rise differed sharply from that of our other corporate examples. There were no exciting technological breakthroughs of the sort that triggered Curtiss-Wright's volatile movements, nor were the company's successes and setbacks as dramatic as those of Winnebago Industries, which are described in the next chapter. Rather, General Mills made news in the mundane way that most corporations do. It issued annual and quarterly reports of sales and earnings, declared dividends, held annual meetings of shareholders, submitted to an interview on its prospects with a reporter for the Dow Jones News Service and the *Wall Street Journal*, made a small acquisition, staged a secondary offering of common stock, and dispatched its executives to speak before various groups of security analysts. Its only direct involvement in any news of national importance came early in 1972, when it was cited in a government action that alleged it was part of a "shared monopoly" of the breakfast cereal industry.

With the latter exception, none of the news stories in which General Mills figured made large headlines, but all contributed to the fundamental reappraisal of the company and its prospects that fueled its stock price rise. Like our previous corporate example, all of the key facts that contributed to the advance were readily available in the public prints. No crystal ball or inside information were required to see them.

The Background

For all of its conservatism and the seemingly unchanging nature of its best-known products, General Mills had undergone a drastic transformation in the decade that ended with the conclusion of its May 30, 1971, fiscal year. The company had entered the 1960s as a commodity-centered concern that milled flour for commercial sale and produced flours, cereals, and cake mixes for home consumption and animal feeds for use on the nation's farms. Only 40% of its sales in 1960 were in consumer markets. Most of the rest were to the agricultural and baking industries, and these had fallen on hard times at the start of the new decade. As a result, the company's profit margins had begun shrinking dangerously.

The first phase of General Mills' changeover began in 1961, when General Edwin Rawlings became the corporation's president. The general had been brought into the company two years before by Charles Bell, who had served under him in the Air Force's Materiels Command. In the service, General Rawlings had gained a reputation as a cool, no-nonsense administrator. This and the fact that he was a newcomer to the company helped him inaugurate a much-needed housecleaning. In short order, he liquidated the money-losing animal feeds division, cut back sharply on commercial grain milling, and sold off an ill-fated venture into home appliance manufacturing. The moves cut into sales but boosted profits considerably in the early 1960s.

"Everybody knew what needed to be done, but it took an outsider to do it," one long-time General Mills executive told the *Wall Street Journal* some years later. "We had become soft in terms of objectivity. Personal relations between executives stood in the way of progress."[2]

General Rawlings then launched the second phase—an acquisition program based around the company's solid marketing position with housewives and children. It eventually brought the company into toys, games, and crafts products (Parker Brothers, Kenner, Rainbow Crafts, and Craftmaster); the fast-growing snack foods field (Tom Huston Peanuts, Morton Foods, Cherry-Levis Foods, and others); and seafoods (Gorton Corp.). The exploits of "the general at General Mills" were the subject of feature stories in *Business Week*, *Newsweek*, *Forbes*, and other publications.

Jim McFarland continued the acquisitions program when he took over as chief executive, though at a slower pace. He took the company into sportswear, with the 1969 purchase of David Crystal Inc., and restaurants, with the 1970 acquisition of Red Lobster Inns, a small chain of seafood eateries in the South.

By the start of fiscal 1969, almost 80% of the company's sales were in consumer markets. The third phase of the long-range plan —consolidation and growth from within—was scheduled to begin. The company's stated objective was a compound annual earnings growth rate of 10%.

However, those gains in per-share profits weren't forthcoming for a number of reasons. One was that in the midst of all its expansion-by-acquisition of the previous years, General Mills had neglected to introduce the kind of new breakfast cereals that were essential to success in the fast-moving field. Another blow to cereal profits resulted from testimony before a U.S. Senate subcommittee in July 1970 that cast doubt on the nutritional value of ready-to-eat cereals in general and those of General Mills in particular. Cheerios was ranked by a widely quoted expert as a soggy 25th among the 60 major cereals evaluated for nutritional value, while Wheaties was a soggier 29th.

Also during this period, the company experienced serious difficulties in consolidating its toys, games, and crafts acquisitions into the general corporate framework. Management controls were particularly lacking in the important Kenner toys unit, where a performance contract with the previous owners had prevented the institution of cost-cutting measures. Pre-tax profits in the division as a whole faded from $10 million in fiscal 1969 to a mere $1.4 million in fiscal 1971.

There were other problems, too. Debt rose sharply during the period and so did interest expenses. The company's number of outstanding common shares climbed from 15.3 million at the end of fiscal 1967 to almost 20 million at the end of fiscal 1971 as a result of acquisitions, making it more difficult to show per-share earnings gains. Beginning in 1968, the company had launched several test vehicles for a planned entry into the restaurant business, and these were showing small but pesky losses. Finally, but not unimportantly, the sluggish business conditions surrounding the 1969–70 recession cut into every phase of corporate activity.

By the start of fiscal year 1972, however, General Mills had taken steps to remedy its problems. Some of these steps were spelled out by Mr. McFarland in a May 1971 interview with the Dow Jones News Service and the *Wall Street Journal.* Among them were the combination of Kenner and Rainbow Crafts, designed to reduce overhead expenses of both (the performance pact with Kenner's ex-owners had ended), a concentration of restaurant efforts around the Red Lobster Inns chain, and an accelerated pace of new cereal and packaged-food product introductions. The executive predicted a 10% per-share earnings gain in fiscal 1972.

Wall Street, however, had heard that song before, and fiscal 1971 results, which were to show a scant 5% profit gain over 1970 to $1.98 a share, weren't released until June 29. Thus, the stock remained stagnant through midyear.

The upward move of General Mills' stock, which was to continue through calendar 1972, began in November 1971. It resulted from a combination of what the company said it would do, what security analysts said it would do, and what actually occurred. To attempt to make those elements clearer we will arrange them in chronological order beginning in late September 1971, two months before the rise commenced.

General Mills in the News

The following stories, presented in condensed form, are dated by their appearance in the *Wall Street Journal*. Many of them appeared on the Dow Jones and Reuters news tickers the day before. Many of them also were carried by the Minneapolis *Tribune* and *Star* in General Mills' home city and by other major newspapers around the country.

September 22, 1971—General Mills announced at its annual meeting that earnings in the 1972 fiscal first quarter were $12.8 million, up 11% from the same period the previous year. Per-share net rose 9.5% to 57 cents from 52 cents. Sales advanced by 13% to $305.2 million. President James A. Summer said the company was "on target" in achieving its goal of an earnings gain of more than 10% for the year.

December 17, 1971—Second quarter earnings of $16.3 million, or 73 cents a share, were announced. That was about 20% higher than the $13.5 million, or 61 cents a year, of a year earlier. Sales in the quarter rose 16.8%. First-half per-share net of $1.30 topped the 1971 figure by 15%. Chairman McFarland said the company's toys, games, and crafts division showed "significant improvement" in the half, and so did Red Lobster Inns. However, he cautioned that second-half gains probably wouldn't match those of the first six months.

January 25, 1972—The Federal Trade Commission accused the nation's four largest cereal makers— Kellogg, General Mills, General Foods, and Quaker Oats—of comprising a "shared monopoly" in their industry, and threatened to break them into smaller units. The *Wall Street Journal* said the move "could prove to be the most significant government anti-trust action in decades," but noted that the FTC "has a long way to go before it proves, if it ever does, that existing law can be used against shared monopolies." The companies denied employing monopolistic practices.

February 28, 1972—Mr. McFarland, after a regular monthly meeting of his board of directors, announced that the company had experienced a substantial improvement in overall business trends in the fiscal third quarter ending that day, and that earnings in the period would top year-ago figures by a minimum of 25%. He also announced the board's approval of write-offs in fiscal 1972 that would reduce earnings by not more than $7.2 million, or 32 cents a share. These resulted from decisions to reduce food plant capacity and close unsuccessful food service and restaurant test ventures. "These moves should benefit fiscal 1973 earnings by at least 10 cents a share and will release substantial capital for rapidly expanding parts of the company," he said.

March 15, 1972—General Mills will earn about $2.30 a share in fiscal 1972 before write-offs, up about 16% from fiscal 1971, Mr. McFarland said in an interview with Dow Jones and the *Wall Street Journal*. Third quarter net was 50 cents against 39 cents in the same period the previous year, a 28% gain. The fourth quarter would be "very good" but not as good as the third quarter, he said.

March 20, 1972—Third-quarter earnings were officially announced. Sales in the period rose by 20%. Nine-month net totaled $40.1 million, or $1.80 a share, up about 19% from $33.7 million, or $1.52 a share, in the 1971 period. Nine-months' sales climbed 17% to $982.7 million.

June 26, 1972—Earnings for the fiscal year ended May 28 were released. They totaled a record $52.2 million, or $2.33 a share, before a write-off of $6.8 million, or 30 cents a share. Net from operations was up about 18% from fiscal 1971. Sales for the year were a record $1.3 billion, a 17.5% gain. Fourth-quarter per-share earnings were 53 cents, a 15% rise from the 1971 quarter. The company increased its quarterly dividend to 25 cents a share from 24 cents.

President Summer said the biggest year-to-year profit gains were registered by the toys division, Red Lobster Inn, and international food operations. Mr. McFarland forecast further profit gains in fiscal 1973. The company's "strong upward momentum" is continuing, he said.

July 24, 1972—General Mills agreed to acquire Kimberly Knit Wear Inc., a New York-based maker of women's knitted apparel, for about $30 million in common stock. The acquisition will add "several cents a share" to fiscal 1973 earnings, Mr. McFarland said.

August 21, 1972—The company released its 1972 annual report, which revealed that capital spending in fiscal 1973 would total $65 million, up from $51 million in 1972. Much of the money would be spent on new product introductions and expansion of retail activities, the report said.

September 20, 1972—At its annual meeting, the company said that profits in the first quarter of fiscal 1973 equaled 68 cents a share, up 19% from the 57 cents of the fiscal 1972 quarter. Sales in the period also rose 19%.

September 25, 1972—The company registered a 550,000-share secondary offering of common stock with the Securities and Exchange Commission. The stock was part of 720,000 shares it paid to acquire Kimberly Knit Wear from its sole owner. All proceeds of the sale would go to Kimberly's former owner.

September 29, 1972—The company asked Price Commission approval of a 9.73% boost in the price of family flour, citing higher wheat costs resulting from the U.S.–Russian grain deal of two months before.

October 4, 1972—The secondary offering of 530,000 shares went to market at $51.75 a share and sold out.

October 7, 1972—The Price Commission okayed the requested flour price boost.

November 1, 1972—The Price Commission okayed a 5.94% increase in the price of General Mills' baking mixes; the company had requested a boost of 6.13%.

December 20, 1972—Second-quarter earnings equal to 92 cents a share, up 24% from 1972's 74 cents, were announced. First-half earnings of $1.61 a share topped the year-ago period by 22% on a 19.5% sales gain to $810.8 million. Mr. McFarland appeared before the New York Society of Security Analysts and said that prospects for meeting the earnings growth rate goal of 10% "appear favorable." He said the company planned to accelerate new product introductions and open more Red Lobster Inns. Growth of the toys division will be "above average," he said.

General Mills and the Analysts

Like most companies its size, General Mills actively sought to keep the investment community informed of its operations and prospects through frequent contacts with security analysts, and the 1971–72 period was no exception. Between mid-1971 and the end of 1972, company executives appeared before analysts' groups in New York, Chicago, Minneapolis, Boston, Tampa, and London, in both formal and informal sessions. In addition, analysts paid numerous visits to company headquarters to talk to officials or phoned its public relations department with specific questions.

By and large, the company's formal presentations to analysts groups, made by Chairman McFarland or Executive Vice Presidents E. Robert Kinney and H. Brewster Atwater, followed a similar pattern. They traced the company's long-term conversion to a consumer-oriented marketing strategy, emphasized the growing importance of nonfood items in its sales and earnings picture and restated the fact that General Mills had ended its all-out acquisitions program and intended to seek future growth from established product lines. The sales and earnings projections contained in the talks were the same as those that had previously been released to the press and shareholders; to do otherwise would violate SEC rules.

The company's talks to analysts, however, went more deeply into the outlook for particular product lines than did general news releases and press interviews. This stemmed mostly from the fact that product-line breakdowns and estimates are a standard part of analysts' reports, while the business press rarely goes into such detail. Product-line information proved to be especially valuable in assessing General Mills' performance before and during its stock price surge, however; its profit gains consisted in good measure from the success of three new cereals introduced in 1971— BucWheats, Frankenberry, and Count Chocula—and from the overwhelming and somewhat surprising success of Hamburger Helper, a quick-meal product that turned in sales of some $25 million in its introductory year. The progress of these lines received scant attention in the company's general news releases.

Analysts had begun sniffing-out General Mills as a potential winner fairly early in 1971. On March 11 of that year, when the stock was selling for $34 a share, a Chicago-based analyst for Mitchell, Hutchins & Co. of New York reported that while fiscal 1971 results would continue to fall short of company goals because of unsatisfactory toy division results, consolidations in that division promised to right things and bring fiscal 1972 and 1973 earnings more in line with expectations. He projected earnings of $2.20 a share in fiscal 1972 and $2.40 in fiscal 1973, and recommended that stock as "a relatively low risk situation for longer-term appreciation."

It was a few months before the bandwagon picked up steam. In May 1971, General Mills executives and analysts attended informal regional sessions sponsored by two brokerage firms that follow the food industry closely—William Blair & Co. of Chicago and Oppenheimer & Co. of New York. On May 20, Blair produced a lengthy report on the company, recommending it as an "above average attraction" at its then current price of about $33 a share. Blair, too, focused on the toy turnaround as the key factor in the expected upsurge and predicted a resulting increase in the company's price-earnings multiple in the months ahead.

The report of Oppenheimer's respected John C. Maxwell, which got into circulation in July, reached very much the same conclusions, even though the stock was still rooted in the mid-thirties. The company "now seems to have gotten most of its problems under control," he wrote in a buy recommendation.

A few more buy reports followed the release of the company's first-quarter earnings, which prompted some analysts to increase their estimates of fiscal 1972 profit to $2.25 a share from $2.20. Perhaps the most timely of these was turned out by Mesirow & Co. of Chicago. Its buy recommendation of October 28, when the stock was at $36, preceded by about three weeks the start of the major run-up.

It wasn't until second-quarter profits were in that most analysts were won over, however. Among the large houses that recommended General Mills to their customers in early 1972 were Kidder Peabody & Co., Merrill Lynch, Burnham & Co., and First Manhattan Co. The buy reports continued throughout the year, although in the later months of 1972, as the stock approached $60 a share, several firms' analysts circulated hold recommendations privately to their salesmen, as is the custom with such reports.

As each new quarterly earnings report was released from Minneapolis, analysts jacked up their estimates of full-year profit for fiscal 1972 and 1973. Inspection of some 30 reports on the company published between mid-1971 and the end of 1972 revealed no instance in which an earnings forecast was revised downward. Generally speaking, analysts in mid-1971 were predicting earnings from operations of $2.20 a share in fiscal 1972 and $2.40 in fiscal year 1973. By late that year, the estimates had risen to $2.25 and $2.50. They were $2.30 and $2.60 in the spring of 1972. Fiscal 1973 estimates rose to $2.70 a share by summer and $2.80 by winter. They actually came in at $2.80.

When the Stock Moved and Why

As Chart 12-1 shows, the first serious upward movement of General Mills' stock came in the final week of November 1971, some three weeks before the announcement of second-quarter results. As we have seen, analysts had been issuing buy recommendations for several months previous to that time, and the company had announced a favorable first quarter on September 22, but the stock remained unmoved. Why? "The company had been talking about 10% annual earnings increases for at least two years, but something always happened to prevent it," said an analyst who followed the company. "The first quarter was a good sign, but it wasn't enough to overcome a credibility gap that had developed. Around the end of the second quarter [November 28], the word out of Minneapolis was that things were on schedule. That's when the stock took off."

Thus, the initial move—from $34 to about $39—resulted from the pros' anticipation of a favorable second quarter. But the

Chart 12-1. General Mills

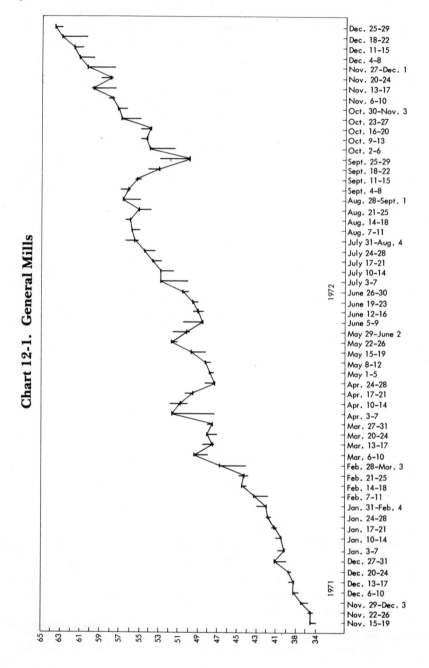

announcement itself, which came on December 16, hadn't been fully discounted. The stock opened that day at $39.25 and tacked on more than two points by year-end.

From there, the stock advanced slowly but steadily until the February 28 announcement of the sizable third-quarter profit gain and the $7.2 million write-off. In only one day between January 1 and February 28 did the stock fluctuate by more than a point, but the news release sparked a rise from $44 to $49 in just two weeks, an 11% gain. General Mills' shares climbed in eight of the nine days immediately following the announcement. The bad news of the write-off had been more than offset by its asserted contribution to 1973 results.

Mr. McFarland's March 15 interview with Dow Jones, in which he placed full-year earnings at $2.30 a share, produced no noticeable reaction on Wall Street; analysts already had been predicting that figure. Likewise nil was the reaction to the March 20 announcement of the third-quarter earnings that the company had revealed three weeks before.

During the week of April 3–7, however, General Mills' stock vaulted again, registering a gain of more than $4 a share for an April 7 close of $51.625. The company made no news in that week, but on April 4, Merrill Lynch issued its buy recommendation on the stock. It wouldn't be farfetched to assume that the giant brokerage firm's report, backed by its sales force of some 5,000, did the trick.

From then until late June, General Mills' stock slipped slightly, mostly hovering between $47 and $49 a share. The sell-off can be attributed to capital gains profit-taking by persons who had bought in during the turn-of-the-year rally six months before. The company made no newsworthy comments or moves during this time.

The stock moved up again with the company's June 26 announcements of full-year earnings, a dividend increase, and the prospect of continuing gains in fiscal 1973. Since the earnings figure already had been forecast by the company and analysts, the latter two factors obviously had the greater impact. From a June

23 (Friday) close of $49.625, the stock moved to $52.75 on July 7. It posted net gains for seven of the next eight weeks, closing on September 1 at $56.75 a share. There is no evidence that the June 26 announcements had been anticipated. The stock moved up a bare ⅝-point the week before it took place.

General Mills' shares suffered their most severe setback of the year between September 5 and 29, dropping from almost $57 to slightly under $50. This came despite the company's announcement of sharply higher first-quarter profit. Three possible explanations for the drop present themselves. First, the stock market as a whole was in decline during the period. Second, the price of wheat, a key commodity that General Mills buys, was on the rise as a result of unexpectedly large Soviet grain purchases. Third was the registration of the secondary offering, which has a generally depressing influence on a company's shares.

Once the secondary was out of the way the stock righted itself, marching solidly upward through the rest of the year. As outlined earlier, General Mills obtained price increases for its wheat products in October and November, and in mid-December announced a whopping gain in second-quarter net. The stock rose almost three points between that announcement at year-end. The late-year profit taking, which hits many stocks whose price is on the upswing, didn't take place.

Perhaps the most important piece of news involving General Mills that had no noticeable effect on its stock was the FTC's anti-trust action. Past experience with such suits had shown that the time gap between the filing of the government's complaint and any move to adjudicate it had been wide indeed. This was the reaction of the investment community. "It is our opinion that the most likely sequence of events is a very lengthy period of litigation, perhaps spanning several years," Merrill Lynch wrote in its April recommendation of the stock. "During that time, we do not foresee any major change in the structure of the cereal industry" or General Mills' position in it.

Summary and Conclusions

The most obvious thing that can be said about General Mills' stock performance during our period of study is that the news about the company was consistently good, and the market responded to it in a uniformly favorable way. Developments that could have been bad—the year-end write-off, the rise in grain prices, and the FTC anti-trust action—either were offset by good news or seemed too distant to pose an immediate threat.

A further and more important point must be made, however. The news concerning the company was *consistently better than what had been expected.* The Niederhoffer-Regan study isolated this as a key factor in the market performance of the big winners of 1970. "The common characteristics of companies registering the best price changes included a forecast of moderately increased earnings and a realized profit gain far in excess of analysts' expectations," they wrote.[3] This description certainly fits General Mills in 1971–72.

The prime source of the over-conservatism about General Mills' profit in fiscal 1972 and the first two quarters of fiscal 1973 was the company itself. The most notable example of this was Mr. McFarland's statement of December 1971 that second-half earnings probably wouldn't match first-half gains; as it turned out, they exceeded them. The company also erred on the side of conservatism in smaller ways. The plant-closing write-offs that were advertised at 32 cents a share came to just 30 cents; the fiscal 1972 third-quarter gain was 28% instead of the predicted 25%; full-year earnings were three cents a share higher than the company forecast. Midway through fiscal 1973, Mr. McFarland still was talking about annual earnings increases of about 10% while actual results were running at more than twice that.

Conversations with General Mills' executives indicate that the practice of underestimating future earnings was partly intentional—the company had been burned previously for over-optimism. It was partly unintentional, too; new products introduced during the period honestly outstripped expectations.

Wall Streeters say that a company can't get away with excessive modesty indefinitely; eventually, it is taken into account in analysts' forecasts. In 1972, however, the practice worked out well for all concerned with General Mills. At least, no one was heard to complain. The same cannot be said of those who participated in the 1972–73 stock market saga of our next corporate specimen, Winnebago Industries.

Notes

1. Frederick C. Klein, "The Road to the Top," *Wall Street Journal*, September 14, 1971, p. 1.
2. Ibid.
3. Victor Niederhoffer and Patrick J. Regan, "Earnings Changes, Analysts' Forecasts and Stock Prices," *Financial Analysts Journal*, May–June, 1972, p. 65.

13

Winnebago Industries: The Road Down

I̲ᴛ was hardly possible to drive along a major highway in the early 1970s without passing a Winnebago motor home. They were hard to miss with their snout-nosed, boxy profiles, and the "flying W" emblazoned on their sides. In many campgrounds, the self-propelled Winnebagos outnumbered the tents, trailers, and other modes of roughing it, twentieth-century style. Inside their Winnebagos, pampered campers luxuriated in air conditioning, cooked in a kitchen outfitted with sink, gas stove, wall oven, and refrigerator, used a private bathroom with shower, and stretched out on real beds to watch color television or listen to stereo tapes.

"I came here to relax, not to be uncomfortable," one Winnebago camper told a *New York Times* reporter, who concluded that "the camper of the nineteen-seventies is not trying to get away from it all—he's trying to take it all with him."[1]

It also was hardly possible to follow the stock market in 1971 and the first half of 1972 without noticing Winnebago Industries,

Inc. The company's stock, first listed on the New York Stock Exchange on September 9, 1970, was the top gainer on the Big Board in 1971, soaring 462% from an adjusted $8.625 at the end of 1970 to $48.50 12 months later. It kept climbing in 1972, hitting $96 a share before a 100% stock dividend was distributed in late June.

Wall Street was in love with leisure. The way the analysts figured it, more take-home pay, longer vacations, and more three-day weekends added up to a bonanza for companies catering to free-time activities. Winnebago was one of the best plays because it was the leader in the fast-growing motor home segment of the recreational vehicle industry, which in turn comprised a big chunk of the leisure market.

But in the second half of 1972, Winnebago stock headed down, even while the company was reporting increased earnings and production. The autumn market surge buoyed the stock a bit, but Winnebago hit its low for the year as the Dow Jones Industrial Average closed above 1,000 for the first time. The decline continued into 1973, and by the end of June the stock had fallen to just $5 a share.

What took the glamor out of Winnebago? Security analysts cited all sorts of reasons, while at the same time insisting that "the fundamentals remain sound." The reasons ranged from the simple fact that Winnebago was a high-priced, volatile stock and thus susceptible to sharp reactions to such specifics as a $445.6 million breach-of-contract suit brought against the company by a former distributor.* What more completely explained the drop, though, was that the news about the company turned from positive to negative during 1972.

Forest City Makes Good

Curtiss-Wright and General Mills, our two previous corporate examples, were venerable companies by American standards when they made their stock market splashes in 1972, but Winnebago was

---

*The suit was eventually settled for $4 million and by early 1973 had lost whatever influence it had on Winnebago's stock.

very much a new firm. The company was formed in 1958 as a result of the efforts of little Forest City, Iowa (population 2,800), to pull itself out of a lingering period of economic stagnation.

Faced with a decline in local farming and a scarcity of industrial jobs to take up the slack, Forest City formed an economic development commission to attract new industry to its area. It built a plant on the outskirts of town and lured a California travel trailer manufacturer to operate it. The venture, known as Modernistic Industries of Iowa, lost money from the start and folded after a few months.

Enter John K. Hanson, a local undertaker and furniture dealer. He acquired the $50,000 property for $12,000 and agreed to run it for a year. This time the company survived, and in 1961 it changed its name to Winnebago Industries after the county in which Forest City is located.

Winnebago, which employed 17 people in 1959, had 3,500 employees by the end of 1972. They worked in a huge central facility of more than two million square feet and in several smaller buildings on a 404-acre tract of former cornfields. In fiscal 1966 (the company's fiscal year ends on the last Saturday in February), when Winnebago went public, the company had sales of $4.4 million and profit of $182,552. By the end of fiscal 1973, those figures had grown to $212 million and $19.4 million, respectively.

Winnebago's stock was split or 100% stock dividends were declared seven times in as many years. By 1973, each share of the 1966 offering had grown to 320 shares, and at the stock's peak in June 1972, an original investment of $1,000 was worth more than $1 million. The Hanson family holdings had grown to about $773 million.

There were about 25 paper millionaires in Forest City (population up to 4,400) in 1972 as a result of Winnebago's stock performance. Some of them lived quietly with their fortunes, but others, along with some not-quite-millionaires, began to live it up. Many of them caught the speculative fever and began plunging into uranium stocks and such. "I'm afraid we have too many speculators and not enough investors," John Martin, president of the Forest City Bank and Trust Company, told the *Des Moines Register*. "People in Forest City believe that anything they buy that doesn't double in value in 30 days is not a good stock."[2]

The wealth to which the residents of Forest City had become accustomed could be traced to a couple of key moves that Winnebago made in its formative years. One was to emphasize motor homes rather than travel trailers and campers, on the hunch that many Americans would answer the call of the wilds as luxuriously as their incomes would allow. In fiscal 1967, motor homes accounted for only 28% of Winnebago's sales, compared to 39% for travel trailers and camper coaches and 33% from the sale of materials and parts. By fiscal 1971, motor homes had ballooned to 90% of the company's greatly increased volume. In 1972, Winnebago had captured an estimated one-fourth to one-third of that lucrative market.

The other move was less conspicuous but just as important. Most recreational vehicle makers patterned their operations after the manufacturers of mobile homes (the kind of vehicles that are towed to trailer courts and parked as more or less permanent residences)—they primarily were assemblers of prefabricated components bought from suppliers, and they tended to build their plants close to the geographical markets they planned to serve. By contrast, Winnebago decided to build all its products in its main plant so as to benefit from economies of scale. It also embarked on a program to build its own components, and by 1972 all it bought from suppliers were chassis, appliances, and power units.

"Why should we give a supplier a profit when we can make a profit?" John K., as he is known around Forest City, was quoted as saying in the June 1, 1972, issue of *Forbes*. Indeed, as a result of central manufacturing and highly integrated production, Winnebago's pre-tax profit margin was nearly 20% of sales in fiscal 1972, against a range of 5% to 11% for its closest competitors.

There were other factors that contributed to the company's success, of course. Its design and production technicians were innovative. Its marketing people set up a sound dealer franchise program. Its executives kept on top of rapid expansion without overburdening the company with debt.

All of which added up to the most important consideration for investors—when consumers' urges to splurge shifted to motor homes, Winnebago was ready to take full advantage.

Going Up

Chart 13-1 shows the performance of Winnebago stock from the time it came on the Big Board in the late summer of 1970 to June 1972. It shot up meteorically during almost the entire 22-month period.

The news was almost all good during that time, and the main good news was that motor homes were selling like beer on a hot day. Winnebago's profit in fiscal 1972 zoomed farther and faster than anyone had imagined. Earnings for the period totaled $13.6 million, or 56 cents a share after adjustment for the later 100% stock dividend, a 195% rise from fiscal 1971. Sales of $133.2 million topped the previous year by 88%.

The final 1972 profit figure was almost double the early estimates of many security analysts, who had to revise their projections upward with each of Winnebago's interim reports. As was

Chart 13-1. Winnebago's Rising Stock
(End-of-Month Closing Prices, Adjusted for 100% Stock Dividends in September 1971 and June 1972)

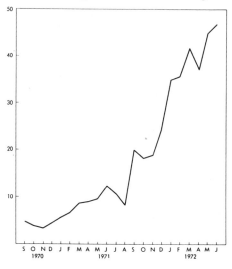

the case with General Mills, this helped to fuel the stock's rise, as did big-block purchases by institutional investors eager to recover from their performance debacle of 1969–70.

On page 11 of its 1972 annual report, Winnebago told how it contributed to the flow of favorable news during the year. "Programs with magazines, newspapers, television and radio stations, free-lance writers and outdoor writers have enabled Winnebago to maintain a preeminent news position in the industry," the company said. "The Winnebago approach continues to focus on the concept and conveniences of 'motor homing' rather than the individual advantages of a Winnebago vehicle." The company believed that as the industry leader, it stood to gain most from any attention the field received.

The only real bad news in 1971 was the announcement that mighty General Motors was *considering* entering the motor home field. GM confirmed the move in February 1972. John V. Hanson, Winnebago's president and the son of John K., the chairman, said that GM's action wouldn't have much effect on Winnebago but might force some smaller producers out of business. "GM's decision to enter the motor home market confirms our belief that the future of the motor home business is good," he said in a statement of February 7. "In the long haul, the GM entry will help the market to expand."

Wall Street bought that argument. Winnebago's stock dipped only slightly before resuming its rise.

In spring, Winnebago made an announcement of its own. It was entering the burgeoning van-type motor home market with a unit called the Minnie Winnie. The move appeared to strengthen the company's position in the industry and help ensure continued rapid growth.

At its annual meeting of May 25, 1972, Winnebago officials predicted that 1973 first-quarter results would set a record. On June 20, the company announced that sales in the period jumped 80% from the year-ago quarter, and that earnings rose 89%. In a statement accompanying the first-quarter report, Gerald E. Boman, chairman of the executive committee, chief executive officer, and John K.'s son-in-law, voiced assurance that the momentum of fiscal 1972 was being maintained. ". . . we have a good product and we offer the best values in the industry," he declared. "For these reasons, we continue to be optimistic about the balance of the selling season and the model year."

But it was not to be. The stock had already peaked at $48.25 six days earlier.

Going Down

Chart 13-2 shows the performance of Winnebago stock from June 1972 through June 1973. The decline was hesitant at first, but definite by autumn. The early December rally didn't last and the stock resumed its descent. Bad news dogged it all the way down.

One of the first elements of bad news was a growing concern about the safety of recreational vehicles. Some articles in this vein appeared in the press in late 1971 and early 1972 in such newspapers as the St. Louis *Post-Dispatch*, but they didn't affect Winnebago's stock, possibly because investors had seen auto sales boom

Chart 13-2. Winnebago's Falling Stock (Adjusted for 100% Stock Dividend in June 1972)

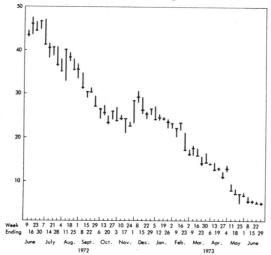

despite safety attacks and thought that recreational vehicles would show similar resiliency.

The concern over safety became more widespread and more frequently reported with the coming of the 1972 camping season. It blossomed on a national scale with a story that appeared in the July issue of *Saga* magazine. *Saga* doesn't normally move the market (or write about business subjects, for that matter) but this time it did, probably because of the sensational and sharply pointed nature of its "exposé." The title of the piece was "Wreckreational Vehicles—Deathtraps on Wheels." In bold-face type beneath the headline came this: "Shockingly, many manufacturers are not only turning out such poorly designed, improperly engineered, and haphazardly overloaded vehicles that they're nothing more than bizarre motor hearses, but when asked by the government about their specifications and load rating, a number wrote back, sorry, they didn't have the slightest idea. Nor did they seem to give a damn that many thousands were destined to be killed or maimed in·glorified fiber glass coffins."

The article didn't come down especially hard on Winnebago, but mentioned that its type of construction didn't employ steel framing, which some of its competitors used. "Which design is safer? Anybody's guess," the article said. "No one has done any rollover testing to find out. And when they flip over, how about body strength? Well, the distributor of one of the most expensive lines of motor homes has privately declared that most of them are *'nothing but oversized cardboard boxes on wheels. In a crash they turn to kindling.'* "

That issue of *Saga* hit the newsstands on July 6. In the first two weeks of July, Winnebago's stock dropped 18% from $47 to $38.375. By the end of the month the stock had slipped 4% more to $36.75.

Winnebago responded to the allegations by initiating impact and rollover tests of its motor homes. In a news release dated August 30, the company said "such testing will become a continuing and integral part of Winnebago's product design program," indicating that it theretofore hadn't been. The bulk of the two-page statement described the company's "long record of concern" for the safety of its products' users.

But that wasn't enough. On September 12, the *Wall Street Journal*'s "Heard on the Street" column, which previously had aired *Saga*'s charges, focused on a negative analysis of Winnebago by Blyth Eastman-Dillon & Company.

> Patrick Sheehan, Blyth Eastman's specialist on the company, also maintains that the motor home industry is a sitting duck for consumer organizations because of the developing controversy over the inherent safety of motor homes. It's a well-publicized fact that the Department of Transportation is conducting a major study of the recreational vehicle field.
>
> Mr. Sheehan warns of the potential damage to Winnebago's image should general criticism of motor-home construction develop. Cited also are the problems of a possible switch into a sturdier construction (which many analysts think likely); also the increased costs and reserves that it might incur from a more extensive warranty program. Winnebago says it already has increased its warranty on new models, but adds that the incremental costs are "small." . . . Adds one top Blyth Eastman research executive: "I'd be a seller [of Winnebago stock]."

The second piece of bad news, as it turned out, was General Motor's entry into the field. Earlier in 1972, Winnebago's efforts to shrug off GM seemed successful. This exchange took place between a shareholder and John V. Hanson at the company's May 25 annual meeting.

> Q. *Barron's* reported that the entry of General Motors into the motor home business, rather than expand demand for the units, will merely take away our business. Any comments on that?
>
> A. We think that GM's entry into the business will in fact expand Winnebago's business. I saw that they came out with their news release Monday, with a photograph of their motor home; I think they made most of the mistakes that I hoped they'd make.

Eight months later, the company was still giving breezy answers to the same question. Following a company presentation to the Seattle Society of Investment Men on January 26, 1973, a listener asked John K. the following question.

Q. What is your attitude toward the announced entry of General Motors into the motor home business?

A. I think all of us are very happy for it. We're proud they entered the market. While they're fitting into a limited market in a high price range, it adds more prestige to the industry. We are a little country Iowa operation—as Maytag is—and the big bad wolf didn't hurt Maytag very bad; in fact, GM is the one that got in trouble, not Maytag, and we hope we can be a Maytag. Does that answer it?

The fact that the question continued to be asked showed that many investors and analysts weren't reassured. In mid-August 1972, White, Weld & Co. issued a research report on the recreational vehicle industry that was generally favorable, but it contained this caveat, "We believe that GM's entry must be viewed as a significant longer term risk to companies in the motor home field because of its financial and marketing influence and its reputation in the automotive products field. If GM's initial entry is successful, the scope of its involvement could always be expanded at a future time."

Besides being bad news for Winnebago in its own right, news of GM's entry prompted investors to keep a sharp lookout for signs that Winnebago's growth might be slipping.

They didn't have long to wait. On August 30 the company hinted and on September 18 it confirmed that earnings for the second quarter increased 75% from a year earlier to $5 million, or 20 cents a share, on an 81% jump in sales to $52.8 million; first-half sales and earnings increased 80% and 83%, respectively, to record levels.

On the face of it, that seemed like good news. So did John K.'s statement at an August 30 dealers' meeting that the company was "very, very optimistic" about its near and long-term future.

What the company didn't point out, but what analysts with sharp pencils discovered quickly, was that while profits rose in the second quarter, Winnebago's rate of profitability was down. Pretax profit margins in the period declined to 16.4% from 18.9% in the previous year's quarter, and from 20.9% in the fiscal 1973 first quarter. Prodded by the analysts, some of whom worked directly for large institutions, the company attributed the decline to start-up costs for the Winnie Minnie, an above-average number of model changes in its large motor homes, and a moderate shift of demand toward smaller models that had lower profit margins. Also, the company had bumped against Phase 2 controls in its effort to raise prices to offset higher materials costs.

Throughout the fall, analysts revised their earnings estimates downward, which is anathema for a stock. Early projections of 90 to 95 cents a share for fiscal 1973 (versus 56 cents in fiscal 1972) were eventually lowered to 82 to 85 cents.

Then came the third-quarter report, issued January 3, 1973. Earnings barely inched up to $4.1 million from $3.9 million the year before, and earnings-per-share remained flat at 16 cents. Analysts again lowered their per-share estimates for the year, this time to 80 cents a share.

They still were high. Fiscal 1973 profit came in at $19.4 million, or 77 cents a share. Pre-tax profit margins slipped to 16.8% from 19.4% the year before.

John K. still sounded like Mr. Sunshine, though. In a statement accompanying the release of fiscal 1973 earnings, he called the year "a period of enormous accomplishment for Winnebago" and said that improvements that had been instituted "put the company in the most competitive position in which it has ever been."

But other doubts were beginning to form, this time about the continued strong growth of the U.S. economy and the soaring rate of inflation; any consumer entrenchments would bear heavily on the high-priced luxury items that Winnebago made.

And sure enough, on May 4, the company announced a 25% cutback in production to 450 units a week. The New York Stock Exchange halted trading in the stock the afternoon of the statement, a Friday. On Monday, the stock dropped more than three points to $9.625.

This time, John K. was a bit more subdued. "To bring inventories into line with the realities of the marketplace, we need to cut back production to levels consistent with our current projections of the balance of the model year," he said in announcing the move. Reasons for the softness in what was normally the industry's strongest selling period "aren't completely clear," he noted. The market "probably reflects continuing consumer uncertainty, weakness of the dollar in world markets and growing concern about much-discussed fuel shortages." A few days later, the company confessed that its previous statements on its outlook had been "overly optimistic."

It was a habit not easily shaken. On June 6, Winnebago announced a further production cutback—this one amounting to 44%. A day later it said it would lay off 500 to 700 employees reneging its 24-hour-earlier assurance that "further layoffs of personnel aren't anticipated at this point." On June 20, the company reported that earnings in the first quarter of fiscal 1974 dropped 36% to $4 million, or 16 cents a share, from $6.3 million, or 25 cents a share, a year earlier.

Summary and Conclusions

Winnebago's stock price decline can be traced to a spate of bad news from outside the company (the safety controversy, competition from GM, and general economic worries) and from the company itself (lower profit margins, earnings growth, and production).

As was the case with Curtiss-Wright, once the flow of the news involving Winnebago changed from good to bad, even normally favorable developments adopted a negative cast. One example was the company's announcement in September 1972 that it was going to build a new plant in Reno, Nevada. That would have been good news when Winnebago was selling motor homes as fast as it could make them, but in light of the company's multitude of troubles it raised questions about excess capacity and a drain on capital. Construction of the plant was cancelled in the wake of the production cutback.

Another element played an indeterminant role in the decline —the way in which Winnebago handled its news releases, earnings reports, and other communications with the press, shareholders, and analysts. On the one hand, Winnebago was a model of corporate virtue in the *amount* of information it provided. For instance, the company was the first in the United States to mail directly to shareholders its detailed 10-K annual report, which every publicly held concern must file with the Securities and Exchange Commission. In 1972 it launched a monthly bulletin that showed production by types of units and informed the public of any news of consequence involving the company that had occurred. The SEC's disclosure rules were followed to the letter; if the company told an analyst anything, it cranked out a news release and told everybody.

But Winnebago turned not-so-candid in sharing the news of its problems in fiscal 1973. When its second-quarter earnings came out, it omitted any mention of its declining profit margins or rising start-up costs. When *Time* magazine came to inquire about the stock price dive, John V. Hanson claimed "that investors have been worried by reports of disappointing shipments in the 'mobile home' industry and have got that mixed up with Winnebago's 'motor home' business."[3]

The *Wall Street Journal* got a similar response when it phoned to get Winnebago's reaction to the previously cited Blyth Eastman report. Dan Dorfman wrote about the answer he got in the "Heard on the Street" column of September 12.

> John V. Hanson, Winnebago's president, seemed eager to talk about the company. The only areas he placed off-limits were earnings, backlogs, growth prospects and plans to ensure continuing growth. Other than that, he says: "Everything is on course for us."
>
> As for the stock's sharp decline, Mr. Hanson shrugs it off. Says the official, who, on the basis of ownership of some 800,000 shares has a paper loss this year of more than $14 million: "It doesn't make a damn bit of difference to me. It's only paper."

A company's failure to be forthcoming about its problems ignores a basic sentiment of journalists and security analysts. Nothing is so galling as a company head (or anyone else) who won't talk. A concern that is silent while it is doing well might get away with it—its actions speak for themselves. But as we also saw with Curtiss-Wright, once things start to slip, a lack of communications compounds a company's stock-price woes. In the case of Winnebago, early over-optimism completed a fatal equation.

Notes

1. B. Drummond Ayres Jr., "Today's Campers Bring the Comforts of Home to the Out-of-Doors," *New York Times*, August 13, 1972, p. 53.
2. Gordon Gammack, "The Get-Rich-Quick Fever at Forest City," *Des Moines Register*, July 9, 1972, p. 39.
3. "Pampering Campers," *Time*, August 28, 1972, pp. 55–56.

Part V

Conclusion

14

Adding It Up

Now we return to our original question: Does the market react to the news, or doesn't it? We think we have shown that it does, in both general and particular ways.

There are a few more points we can make, however, based on our research for this book and our experience as business journalists. They are as follows:

1. *The news media portray business in a light that's more flattering than it should be.* This, of course, is an observation rather than a conclusion, but it is widely accepted. It stems mainly from the fact that the primary sources of business news—corporations and the federal government—have important stakes in the impression that news creates. Companies relentlessly accentuate the positive in reporting their own affairs and many news outlets are inclined to accept their versions. While the economic statistics compiled by the government are generally judged to be free of political taint, administration officials—for political ends—often try to manipulate their interpretation and the timing of their release.

The tendency to manipulate seems to be strongest when an administration's handling of the economy is at issue.

A contributing factor to the optimistic bias of the news media is the vast preponderance of buy advice that pours out of the nation's brokerage firms (and qualifies as news because it is increasingly being published by the firms themselves and quoted in the general press). It reflects the fact that brokers conduct securities research as an adjunct to their business of buying and selling stocks on behalf of their customers.

In the face of all this, it might be considered remarkable that stocks ever decline at all. That they do frequently is perhaps the prime example of the discounting process that one hears so much about around Wall Street. It also testifies to the ability of investors of all stripes to read between the lines before they reach their buy and sell decisions. But this ability doesn't carry with it the capacity to see into the future.

2. *The market is more responsive to news than it used to be.* This observation is based on three long-term trends: The ever-more-inclusive disclosure rules of the U.S. Securities and Exchange Commission, the growing proportion of stock-trading volume accounted for by institutions, and the increasing emphasis on trading profits instead of dividend income.

The effect of these trends on the individual investor is difficult to determine. Tougher SEC rules mean that companies must announce, publicly and promptly, things that they formerly withheld and that, in consequence, often found their way into circulation as rumors or inside information passed between the well-connected. Wall Streeters agree that rumors and inside information still move stocks, but they play less of a role than they used to.

On the other hand, institutions remain better equipped to get the news more quickly than individuals. They are more likely to subscribe to the business news wire services, they get preferred treatment from brokers, and they aren't distracted by other occupations.

The net result for the individual might well be that he's no better or worse off than before.

3. *There is a flow to the news, and when it is pronounced the market as a whole moves with it.* This is the most general way of stating what we have shown in Chapters 5, 6, and 7. We make this statement with full awareness of the possible inadequacies of our News Index. Besides the limitations already mentioned, we might add that we are able to attach only the most general significance to the numerical values the measure yields. For instance, we wouldn't argue that the news in a week that scores a plus-10 is five times better than a plus-2 week, nor could we observe any relationship between the size of the News Index score and the extent to which the market rose or fell in the period in question.

Still, we don't think our conclusions were arrived at lightly. Our analysis of the news surrounding the eight major market turns of 1966–71 encompassed 97 weeks of daily newspapers, or almost two full years. The addition of the entire year of 1972 raised the total to almost three years.

In each phase of our study, we were able to identify lengthy periods in which the news was distinctly good or bad. The news didn't regularly change character *before* the stock market turned, but once it did turn, both marched in the same direction in all eight periods covered in chapters 5 and 6 and in the year-end rally that sent the DJIA over the 1,000 mark in late 1972. For all of 1972, the news and the market moved in the same direction in 40 of 52 weeks. If one can't find out what *will* happen—and no system yet devised yields that information—it's at least nice to know what's happening while it's going on.

4. *There is a flow to the news regarding individual issues and companies, and the stocks involved tend to move with that flow.*

Examples of this emerge clearly in the chapters on how the war and pollution issues affect stocks and in the chapters that relate how the stocks of three companies reacted to the news that touched them. In all five cases, the stocks involved moved up (down) as long as the *bulk* of the related news was positive (negative), but once the flow turned decisively so did the direction of the stocks, even though individual news items occasionally bucked the current.

The turning points obviously were more apparent in retrospect than they were at the time, but they were nonetheless real. Once the ill effects of the war in Vietnam sank in around mid-1966, escalations of the conflict ceased to exert a bullish impact on stocks. Once the dollar value of pollution control became sufficiently well defined, many pollution control stocks fell from favor, even though bursts of optimism were still to be heard. Curtiss-Wright's stock boomed despite considerable adverse comment until General Motors made its Wankel engine intentions clear, but after that even news items similar to those that boosted the stock previously fell flat. Two consecutive, strong quarterly earnings reports pulled General Mills out of a lengthy stock market rut and into a sustained, 14-month advance. Winnebago stock shook off GM's entry into its field while it was going up, but even the announcement of a major new facilities program (later canceled) couldn't halt its decline.

The notion of a flow to the news about specific stocks requires further study. The idea that stocks have momentum isn't a new one on Wall Street, however, and it helps explain some of the otherwise inexplicable ways stocks react to news.

Suggested Reading

Since little has been written about how news affects stocks, the titles assembled below constitute not the literature of the field but rather source material for bits and pieces of information on the subject.

The Market

Some of the best books for an overall look at how the market operates are anthologies. Three good ones are: *The Anatomy of Wall Street*, edited by Charles J. Rolo and George J. Nelson (Lippincott, 1968); *The Stock Market Handbook*, edited by Frank G. Zarb and Gabriel T. Kerekes (Dow Jones-Irwin, 1970); and *The Wall Street Reader*, edited by Bill Adler and Catherine J. Greene (World, 1970). A few chapters in these books touch on the impact of news on stock prices, but more illuminating information is found in the discussions of market theories and investment strategies.

Robert Sobel's *The Big Board* (Free Press, 1965) gives historical examples of the role news has played in stock market action.

Adam Smith's *The Money Game* (Random House, 1968) offers insight into how the investment game is played by the big institutional investors.

Interpreting the News

Evaluating the meaning and importance of the news can be a problem for an investor. *How Business Economists Forecast*, edited by William F. Butler and Robert A. Kavesch (Prentice-Hall, 1966), is a technical but useful guide to interpreting government statistics, which comprise a good share of each day's business and financial news. A more narrow approach is taken in *Money and Markets: A Monetarist View* (Irwin, 1971) in which economist Beryl Sprinkel interprets monetary statistics in terms of their influence on market action.

In *The Sophisticated Investor: A Guide to Stock Market Profits* (Simon & Schuster, 1964), Burton Crane, who covered Wall Street for the *New York Times*, relates types of news items to his particular brand of investment advice. Many of his buy-and-sell signals appear as items in the business press.

Financial Analysts Journal (The Financial Analysts Federation, bimonthly) is helpful in keeping abreast of what information companies report or don't report and why. A large share of business news emanates from companies, and this periodical is a good place to follow the trend toward fuller corporate disclosure.

Special Study of Security Markets of the Securities and Exchange Commission, Part I (U.S. Government Printing Office, 1963) contains a dated but nonetheless thorough analysis and critique of the investment advisory and security research services. Because these services are the source of some important market-moving news, it is a good idea to be cognizant of their foibles, which this study documents in great detail.

News: A Consumers Guide, by Ivan and Carol Doig (Prentice-Hall, 1972), provides a guide for readers who wish to evaluate the news accurately and objectively. Business and financial news are included, but the book does not focus particularly on these areas.

The Influence of Mass Media

A classic study of how people are affected by what they read and hear is *The People's Choice*, by Paul Lazarsfeld, Bernard Berelson, and Helen Gaudet (Columbia University Press, 1968). Originally published in 1944, the book is now in its third edition. Time hasn't diminished the value of this milestone work, even though the advent of television has made some of its conclusions obsolete.

Public Opinion Quarterly (American Association for Public Opinion Research, quarterly) publishes interdisciplinary articles on elements that shape public opinion, and *Journalism Quarterly* (Association for Education in Journalism, quarterly) occasionally has articles on the influence of the mass media. *Columbia Journalism Review* (Columbia University, bimonthly) publishes critiques of the press, but these usually are on a case-by-case basis and are journalistic rather than quantitative in nature.

Readers who are curious about how good journalists approach reporting financial news may find some insight in *Interpretative Reporting*, by Curtis D. MacDougall (Macmillan, 1963, 4th ed.). This book, also something of a classic in its field, stresses that reporters should emphasize the why behind the who-what-when-where-how formula.

Index